IMPLEMENTING THE NATIONAL NUMERACY STRATEGY

FOR PUPILS WITH LEARNING DIFFICULTIES

Access to the Daily Mathematics Lesson

ANN BERGER, DENISE MORRIS
AND JANE PORTMAN

David Fulton Publishers
London

David Fulton Publishers Ltd
Ormond House, 26–27 Boswell Street, London WC1N 3JD

First published in Great Britain in 2000 by David Fulton Publishers
Reprinted 2000

British Library Cataloguing in Publication Data
A catalogue record for this book is available from the British Library

ISBN 1–85346–664–6

Typeset by Textype Typesetters, Cambridge
Printed in Great Britain by Bell and Bain Ltd, Glasgow

Contents

Acknowledgements

Many teachers have helped to make this book possible. Particular thanks go to teachers in the following Bristol schools

Henbury Manor School
Claremont School
New Fosseway School
Briarwood School
Kingsweston School

Many thanks also to Regent Special School, Oldbury, for some of the number rhymes for older pupils in Appendix 3 and to all the schools who helped us pilot these materials.

Foreword

The government has launched a major drive to raise standards in numeracy by the year 2002; 75 per cent of pupils at the age of 11 must at least achieve level 4 in the tests for mathematics. These targets will be hard to achieve if pupils who are currently identified as having special educational needs do not make faster progress in numeracy. In Bristol we have a major initiative to raise standards across all pupils, not just those likely to attain level 4. We are committed to including all pupils in the National Numeracy Strategy and in the intensive support work we undertake to raise both the quality of teaching and the standards pupils attain in numeracy.

Following the successful programme to support schools in raising standards of literacy, we have embarked this year on another project to work with schools to implement the National Numeracy Strategy for pupils attaining below level 1 of the National Curriculum.

This book aims to publish and spread more widely the work that we have done. Many pupils will work on the same learning objectives for many years and in the scheme of work included in this book we have tried to show how similar learning objectives can be taught in an age appropriate way. In addition we have given much clearer guidance about precisely what needs to be learnt in order to achieve the key reception objectives identified in the National Numeracy Strategy. These key objectives currently contain too many different elements to enable teachers to break down clearly the small steps of learning that need to take place. Related to these component parts of the learning objectives are a wide range of activities and resources to help teachers choose activities which will be motivating and enjoyable for pupils and encourage them to learn more quickly. The activities have been carefully chosen to clearly match the learning objectives identified.

A video and training pack to support this book is available from Bristol City Council, Bristol Education Centre, Sheridan Road, Horfield, Bristol BS7 0PU, telephone 0117 903 1355, or e-mail ann_berger@bristol-city.gov.uk

Richard Riddell
Director of Education, Bristol City Council
January 2000

Bristol City Council has produced a video and training pack based on the materials in this book. It is designed to help subject coordinators provide training in schools. The training pack consists of a range of activities which can be used during staff in-service days. The video consists of mathematics lessons which use the guidance in the National Numeracy Strategy.

It can be obtained by contacting Bristol City Council at Bristol Education Centre, Sheridan Road, Horfield, Bristol BS7 0PU or telephone 0117 903 1355. You can also email ann_berger@bristol-city.gov.uk for further information.

1 Who this book is for and how to use it

Overview

Teachers in a number of different settings may find this book helpful. It is designed to provide guidance on implementing the National Numeracy Strategy (NNS), whether you work in a mainstream or special school setting.

The book is divided into seven chapters.

Chapter 1 describes how this book can be used and how it relates to the NNS framework.

Chapter 2 explains what numeracy means for pupils with special educational needs and the key concepts that need to be taught.

Chapter 3 covers some of the questions our teachers have asked and the guidance we have given. It also considers challenges of including pupils with a wide range of needs within the strategy. It offers guidance on teaching strategies for various types of special needs.

Chapter 4 includes a substantial section on questions that teachers can use to develop pupils mathematically.

Chapter 5 contains a breakdown of the 11 key reception objectives from the NNS into specific learning objectives, which match each of the pre level 1 descriptors (distributed to schools by the Qualifications and Curriculum Authority (QCA) in December 1998). The objectives have been ordered into the four strands of the NNS framework. This will help teachers ensure breadth and balance when planning for mathematics. (Handling data is covered within problem solving.)

Chapter 6 describes examples of activities and resources to teach these objectives to pupils. Resources suitable for pupils at Key Stage 1, 2 and 3 are described.

Chapter 7 contains examples of the way the guidance in this book has been used to support teachers long, medium and short-term planning.

The appendices include other recommended resources and a glossary of terms.

Many teachers have pupils of very differing abilities in one class. Some pupils may be at level 1 or 2 and there may be one or two pupils at much earlier stages. Planning for these classes to ensure progression for everyone is particularly difficult. Teachers can use this book to help their planning by choosing objectives from the NNS framework for pupils working at higher levels and then use Chapter 5 to choose related objectives for pupils working below level 1.

The DfEE has commissioned Bristol City Council Education Department to provide further guidance for the NNS for pupils with special needs and this book supports the use of this guidance and provides further examples to help teachers.

How to use this book

Teachers with pupils working on pre level 1 objectives

After choosing the strand of numeracy that you are going to teach you can use Chapter 2 to ensure you are clear about the key concepts underpinning the learning objectives. Chapter 4 will help you choose key questions to use in your lessons. Chapter 5 will help you choose objectives at the right level for your pupils. Chapter 6 will help you plan appropriate activities and choose resources. Chapter 7 sets out some example plans to help you.

SENCOs and numeracy coordinators

Chapters 2 and 3 will help you to guide other teachers in the school when they ask about classroom organisation, Individual Education Plans (IEPs), using classroom assistants effectively, and a range of other questions. The example plans will help you to choose whole-school formats that suit your individual situation.

Teachers in mainstream classes with a wide range of ability

Chapter 5 breaks down the reception key objectives from the NNS. If you have pupils in your class who are working from objectives from other year groups and other pupils who are working at P levels you can use the book to help plan your lesson. You can choose the objectives for the majority of the class. Then look and see which of the objectives in Chapter 5 are from the same strand. You can then choose objectives that link well together and you are more likely to be able to provide activities that target the whole ability range in your class.

Promoting high standards of numeracy for pupils with special educational needs

On page 4 of the National Numeracy Strategy, a long list of factors have been identified which promote high standards of numeracy across all schools. Many of those factors are important in all schools; however, certain aspects need additional emphasis when teaching pupils with special educational needs.

School management

The head teacher needs to be positively involved in the implementation of the strategy and to be committed to ensuring that daily mathematics teaching for between 45 and 60 minutes is possible in every class. In special schools there are many factors to take into account. Many schools have visiting therapists and a whole range of commitments that take place during the day which make timetabling of the daily mathematics lesson particularly challenging. Schools have been most effective in raising standards where the commitment is there from all members of staff to allocate this time including the commitment of staff from other disciplines.

Training is required for all staff if they are to make this commitment, and training for classroom assistants is particularly important. The programmes designed for classroom assistants during in-service training days have to be very carefully thought through so that they both feel involved in the new initiative as well as having opportunities to discuss and develop their own particular roles. There is a video and training pack to go with this book which includes activities for classroom assistants. It can be obtained from the Bristol Education Centre (see the Foreword to this book).

The way parents are involved within the new project is also important. Many youngsters with special educational needs require their learning to be reinforced very regularly both at home and at school. Parents need to understand very clearly what objectives are being taught and how they are being taught in order that they can continue to take opportunities in the home situation to reinforce numeracy skills, knowledge and understanding. For example, opportunities occur when laying up for dinner, changing and dressing and during the travelling time that is often so lengthy for these youngsters. The training pack also includes activities that can be undertaken during a workshop session for parents.

Curriculum

In relation to **curriculum and assessment** there are also some particularly important factors which need to be considered to promote high standards of numeracy. In particular staff need to share a common understanding of what numeracy is and how best to develop pupils' skills, knowledge and under-standing. This raises a particular challenge for pupils with special educational needs as often pupils at the earliest stages of learning are focusing on objectives that are difficult to define in terms of different curriculum subjects.

Schools need to agree clearly what aspects of numeracy are to be taught and how they are going to be taught, including what aspects of numeracy are reinforced through the curriculum and what aspects are taught discreetly during the daily mathematics lesson. These decisions are very important and need clear whole-school policies if staff are to feel secure and pupils' continuity through the curriculum is to be assured. There is further guidance on this in Chapter 7 on planning.

The National Numeracy Strategy stresses the importance of mental calculation and recall of number facts. This also presents very particular challenges for teachers of pupils with special educational needs. Some of these pupils find communication very difficult and though they may have achieved the mental calculation and can recall the number facts they may be unable to communicate that effectively. A whole range of new strategies need to be developed to enable pupils to communicate their learning quickly and together with other pupils so that time is not wasted while pupils take turns. Further guidance on this is contained in Chapter 3.

Assessment

Individual Education Plans and the learning objectives identified in the curriculum planning for numeracy have to be carefully thought through so that pupils make progress in relation to their specific targets, but also achieve a broad and balanced mathematics curriculum. There is further help on this both in Chapter 7 on planning and in Chapter 3 'The inclusive mathematics lesson'.

Teaching

In relation to **teaching**, better numeracy standards can be attained when teachers structure their mathematics lesson and maintain a good pace. This is also sometimes difficult for pupils with special educational needs who particularly need longer to respond to teachers' questions and within a small classroom may all be working at very different levels. Direct whole-class teaching under these circumstances is sometimes challenging but with careful curriculum planning great progress can be made by all pupils in the way that they are involved in the main teaching activity. There is further help on this in Chapter 3.

There are also many issues that need to be considered in relation to resources for pupils with special educational needs. Many of these youngsters are working on similar objectives for a long period of time and the resources for older pupils are not necessarily available. Many have to be made by teachers and this can be very time consuming. Chapter 6 contains suggested resources suitable for pupils of different age groups.

2 Teaching mathematics

What is mathematics?

Mathematics is about the search for, and the study of, patterns and relationships, often using symbols. The patterns can be number patterns, or shapes, or arrangements.

Mathematics is crucial to a child's understanding of the way the world is ordered. It is a means of communicating information and ideas. It is also a creative activity, involving imagination, intuition and discovery. It is essential for all pupils whatever their ability.

Doing mathematics involves exploring and investigating mathematical systems and operating on these systems in order to find out more about them. It involves applying knowledge, skills and understanding to solve problems in a variety of contexts.

What is numeracy?

The National Numeracy Strategy defines numeracy as:

> a proficiency which involves confidence and competence with numbers and measures. It requires an understanding of the number system, a repertoire of computational skills and an inclination and ability to solve number problems in a variety of contexts. Numeracy also demands practical understanding of the ways in which information is gathered by counting and measuring, and is presented in graphs, diagrams, charts and tables.

What are the key concepts for pupils with learning difficulties?

- the concept of number, including cardinality and ordinality

- the concept of counting, including one-to-one correspondence

- the operation or combining and partitioning

- the concept of comparing two numbers

- the concepts of length, mass, capacity, time and value (money)

- the operation of comparing two quantities

- the classification of 3D solids and 2D shapes

- the concept of a mathematical pattern

- the concept of having properties or attributes

- the concept of classification by criteria

- the concepts of position, direction and movement

A pupil from Claremont School working on the concept of classification by criteria

The National Numeracy Strategy strands

The National Numeracy Strategy includes these concepts in the 11 key objectives for the reception year. They are listed in the NNS Framework for Teaching Mathematics in Section 2, page 2. In this book these objectives have been ordered into the four strands of the NNS.

Strand	Key objectives
1. Numbers and the number system	1, 2, 3, 4a
2. Calculations	5, 6, 7
3. Solving problems	8, 11
4. Measures, shape and space	4b, 9, 10

Key objectives	Key objectives Pupils will be able to . . .
1	Say and use the number names in order in familiar contexts.
2	Count reliably up to 10 everyday objects.
3	Recognise numerals 1 to 9.
4a	Use language such as more or less, greater or smaller, to compare two numbers.
4b	Use language such as more or less, longer or shorter, heavier or lighter to compare two quantities.
5	In practical activities and discussion, begin to use the vocabulary involved in adding and subtracting.
6	In practical activities and discussion, find one more or one less than a number from 1 to 10.
7	In practical activities and discussion, begin to relate addition to combining two groups of objects, and subtraction to 'taking away'.
8	Talk about, recognise and recreate simple patterns.
9	Use language such as circle or bigger to describe the shape and size of solids and flat shapes.
10	Use everyday words to describe position.
11	Use developing mathematical ideas and methods to solve practical problems.

Strand 1: Numbers and the number system

1. The concept of number

The word number relates to the idea of quantity and a given number will tell us how many items there are in a set. One way of thinking about this is to use the idea of 'as many as'. We can say that all sets which have 'as many as' each other have the same number of items. To distinguish between the numbers we give them number names. The number names in English are one, two, three, etc. Each number has a given symbol, which is used to record it. These symbols for number names are called numerals and are written 1, 2, 3, etc. The symbol for the number name of an empty set (zero) is 0 and should be introduced to pupils alongside the other numerals.

The number names and their numerals are fixed labels. In other words, a quantity of four items is always named as four and the numeral 4 is always used to record how many there are in the set. **It is very important for pupils to learn the permanence of these names and numerals, and understand the 'twoness' of two.**

Similarly, **pupils need to learn that the numbers are in a fixed order and this does not change.** Two always follows one and three always follows two.

As numbers tell us how many items there are, their size can be compared. **The concepts of 'more than' and 'fewer than' need to be learnt in relation to quantity.** Pupils need to learn that a set of three items is always more than a set of two items, regardless of the size of the items themselves.

The properties of numbers need to be understood.

- Things have labels and numbers are used to label quantities.

- There are fixed number names and symbols (numerals).

- Numbers are in a fixed order.

---

2. The concept of counting

Learning to count involves learning a range of concepts and skills.

One-to-one correspondence is the concept of a relationship between two sets of items such that every member of the first set is paired with a unique item in the second set. **When learning to count pupils will 'tag' each item once with a number name so that each item is linked to a number.**

Pupils need to learn the cardinality of numbers; in other words the last number names the set and indicates the size of the set.

Strand 2: Calculations

Operating on the number system involves calculating. The concept underlying addition and subtraction is that sets of items can be operated on. They can be **combined** (put together) and **partitioned** (split into parts). Operations form a large part of mathematics and pupils spend a lot of time dealing with simple operations on the number system.

Initially, operations involving numbers need to involve objects. When two sets of objects are combined the number of the combined set can be found by counting. Finding this total is the operation of addition. When one set of objects is removed from a set, the number of the set that is left can be found by counting. Finding the size of the set that is left is the operation of subtraction.

Another aspect of the subtraction operation that needs to be learnt is about comparing the size of two sets. Key questions are 'What is the difference?', 'How many more?', 'How many fewer?'. These can be answered by matching items in each set so that there is one-to-one correspondence and counting those items that do not have a match in the other set.

The operations of combining and partitioning are the inverse of each other and need to be taught alongside each other so that pupils understand that one operation can 'undo' the other.

The operation of addition with whole numbers has the property of being commutative. In other words the order of the numbers being combined does not change the total. The operation of subtraction is not commutative: a change in the order of the two numbers does change the answer.

Strand 3: Solving problems

Solving mathematical problems involves applying knowledge and understanding of systems and of operations in a variety of contexts. Pupils will need to be given the opportunity to develop their problem solving skills. They need to:

- Make decisions about which equipment and resources are the most appropriate to use in particular situations.

- Make decisions about which mathematical operation to use to solve a word problem.

- Make decisions about which method to use to solve the problem.

- Experience open-ended questions which do not imply the method to be used to solve the problem and which may have a range of solutions.

Pupils need to be given the opportunity to become familiar with the processes and strategies of working mathematically and problem solving. These include:

- Planning their own work.

- Making a diagrammatic representation of the problem.

- Searching for a pattern in the results.

- Making a conjecture about the result (a guess or estimate or inference).

- Trial and improvement (refining the method).

- Looking at a simpler related problem.

- Making a prediction about what will happen next.

- Checking for accuracy.

- Generalising and specialising.

- Justifying and explaining their work and the results.

- Evaluating their own work.

Problem solving activities need to be based in a wide variety of contexts which the pupils can relate to. These could be 'real life' situations or role-play contexts.

1. Solving problems about money

The value of an object or of services is usually measured in units of money. In Great Britain we have a decimal system of units, which makes operations easier than it used to be with a non-decimal money system. Pupils need to learn that coins and notes represent different values and that this is **not based on one-to-one correspondence**.

2. Solving problems by looking for mathematical patterns

The essence of algebra is captured in the nature of mathematical patterns, the search for patterns, the creation of patterns and the understanding of relationships between those patterns. The communication of these patterns is also important.

A mathematical pattern is made up from a starting point and a generating rule. A mathematical pattern can be an arrangement of points, lines, shapes, solids or numbers. The starting point is the first item in the series and the generating rule defines how the next items in the series are created. For example, a number pattern 1, 3, 5, 7 . . . has a starting point of 1 and the generating rule is add 2.

To understand the concept of a mathematical pattern, pupils need to experience working in the following ways with a wide variety of materials and resources:

- Copying patterns

- Continuing patterns

- Creating patterns

- Recreating patterns

- Talking about patterns and describe them

- Recognising patterns as mathematical.

Strand 4: Measures, shape and space

1. The concept of comparing two quantities

In the same way that it is possible to compare two numbers and identify which is larger and which is smaller than the other, it is also possible to compare objects according to their properties, or attributes. For example, by comparing the masses of two objects, the one that is heavier than, lighter than, the other can be identified. Pupils need to learn that quantities can be compared by one of their attributes.

There are some attributes that are absolute. In other words these attributes stand two words alone and do not change when the object is compared to other objects: for example, the attribute of shape (it is a circle or it is not a circle) and the attribute of colour (it is red or it is not red). Other attributes are relative, in other words they are judged in comparison to other objects. Examples of relative attributes include mass (it is heavier than or lighter than another is), length (it is longer than or shorter than another is), and capacity (it can contain more than or less than another can).

2. The operation of comparing

In order to compare two quantities according to a given property or attribute, pupils need to learn how to undertake the comparison. This must be distinguished from taking an absolute measurement of the object. When comparing the properties of two objects, the outcomes of the comparison will be to identify which object, in comparison to the other:

Number	is more than, is less than
Length	is longer than, is shorter than
Mass	is heavier than, is lighter than
Capacity	holds more than, holds less than
Area (2D shapes)	is bigger than, is smaller than
Time	is before, is after.

3. Length

Length is a property of both 2D and 3D objects, though it only refers to how long an object is in one dimension. In order to compare two lengths, pupils will need to:

• Understand that length is one dimensional.

• Ensure that the two lengths start at the same place.

- Identify that the two lengths are different.

- Understand that the length which is farther from the starting point is the longer and the other is shorter than the other.

4. Mass (weight)

Mass is commonly referred to as weight. It is the property of an object that determines how heavy the object is at a certain place. In order to compare two masses, pupils will need to use balance scales or their hands as if they were balance scales. Pupils will need to:

- Understand that mass is about heaviness.

- Ensure that the two objects are each placed in a balance pan (or their hands).

- Identify that the two masses are different.

- Understand that the object that makes the balance pan or hand go down farther than the other is heavier than the other is. The object that goes up from the balance point is lighter than the other.

5. Capacity

Capacity is the attribute that refers to the amount that an object can contain. In order to compare two capacities, pupils will need to fill two containers with the same substance (usually water) and identify which container holds more than the other and which holds less than the other.

6. Area

The area of a 2D shape is the amount of space it takes up on a flat surface. This is a two-dimensional measurement and takes account of length and width.

7. Time

When making comparisons of the amount of time taken by incidents or when incidents took place, pupils need to be aware of the passage of time. Pupils need to make the comparison of when an incident took place in relation to another: before or after.

8. Properties of 2D shapes

Two-dimensional flat shapes have several properties which pupils can use to describe them. These include:

- Name

- Number of edges

- Number of angles (vertices)

- Number of straight and curved edges.

9. Properties of 3D solids

Three-dimensional solids have several properties which pupils can use to describe them. These include:

- Name

- Number of faces

- Number of edges

- Number of angles (vertices)

- Number of straight and curved faces.

10. Position, direction and movement

The **position** of two objects in relation to each other can be described as:

over, under, next to, above, below, on, in, outside, inside.

All these concepts need to be learnt by pupils when studying position.

The **direction** of an object in relation to another can be described as:

in front, behind, opposite, apart, between, left, right, up down, along, through, away from.

All these concepts need to be learnt when studying direction.

The **movement** of an object can be described as:

slide, roll, turn, stretch, bend, forwards, backwards, sideways, through.

All these concepts need to be learnt when studying movement.

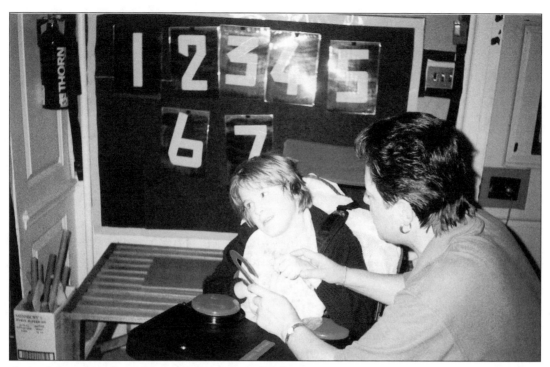

A pupil from Henbury Manor School recognising the numerals 1 and 2 (key objectives 3)
The switch on the pupil's right is programmed to say 'one' and the switch on the left 'two' when pressed. She is being asked to press the correct switch for the number being shown. This pupil is working at P level 5 (See page 34).

3 The inclusive mathematics lesson – your questions answered

The guidance in this section supplements pages 18 to 32 in Section 1 of the NNS Framework for Teaching Mathematics.

> **1. Should we set the pupils for mathematics lessons?**

Many classrooms in special schools and resource bases in mainstream schools have pupils with a very wide range of ability and also pupils of different ages. Some classes have a whole key stage within a class and some have pupils across two and sometimes even three key stages.

This clearly presents many challenges to teachers when planning for differentiation. The most able pupils may well not be the oldest pupils and great care needs to be taken when deciding whether or not to set pupils across a group of classes or group pupils by ability within the classes.

It can be difficult to provide consistency for pupils if they are moving between classrooms and teachers. Often a pupil has to have specialised equipment that has to be moved too, and this can present more challenges. Moving between classrooms can also be very time consuming and taught time is already under considerable pressure. In addition the least able pupils often benefit from being with others working at a higher level. Setting pupils can lead to lower expectations of certain groups and it can reduce opportunities for pupils to 'surprise' us.

These factors need to be balanced against some of the possible advantages. In particular, it might be easier for the teacher to maintain an appropriate pace in the whole-class work if pupils are all of similar ability. Sometimes a group of pupils need to be stretched and this can be easier in setted groups, as the work can be targeted specifically at the level most appropriate for the whole group.

If the school decides to set pupils for mathematics, the age groups of the pupils should not be too far apart so that pupils are working on activities and using resources which are not too 'young' or 'old' for them.

> 2. How can we differentiate during the whole-class session?

Even if teachers have decided to set for mathematics, it is likely that there will still be a wide range of ability in the group. Even when ability levels are similar, pupils' communication strategies may be very different. It is the pupils' ability to communicate their mathematical thinking that presents the greatest challenge when implementing the whole-class teaching session of the NNS. A fundamental principle of the Strategy is that lessons start with a short mental oral activity and that pupils working on objectives up to Year 2 will not be taught standard written methods of calculation. As a result many lessons are taught with much emphasis on dialogue, chanting and quick responses to questions. Pupils who use augmentative communication, signing, eye pointing or other forms of body movement need time to respond and are likely to do so at a different pace. Nevertheless this type of whole-class teaching is essential to maintain the overall pace of the lesson and ensure pupils have opportunities to learn from each others' responses. The following strategies might be helpful to ensure a successfully differentiated mental oral session.

- Choose the quickest form of communication for a pupil even if at other times something more complex is used. For example, a pupil who uses a touch-talker normally may be given digits to touch on their tray for the oral part of the lesson.

- Switch-operated technology may be programmed to produce a selection of answers or a pupil may have to choose between two switches.

- A pupil who eye points may have a limited choice of numbers on a 'washing' line.

- Rows of answer cards that can be placed on a pupil's tray or desk for the pupil to select the correct answer.

The most important aspect of this part of the lesson is that all pupils have a chance to respond.

- Taking turns around the class can be a very slow method of ensuring everyone participates and pupils can become bored or distracted during the process.

- The key is to expect all pupils to answer even if they do so at a different rate.

- When counting up and back encourage chanting as a group rather than taking turns.

- It is essential to plan objectives for pupils at all the ability levels; for example
  - the key objective may be to count on from 1 to 10: Within that there may be other objectives for certain pupils, e.g. to explore 5 balls or to point to 10 objects in a row as the class counts from 1 to 10.

During this time a pupil working on one-to-one correspondence at the earliest levels might have a ball placed on their tray or in their hands so they can explore and feel it. Some pupils may need adult support for this activity.

> **3. How is it best to make use of classroom assistants?**

Classroom assistants have an important role in facilitating the communication in the whole-class oral work.

They are often able to 'read' pupils' minds and can communicate their thinking. However, they should not do the work for pupils. Rather, they should reinforce and encourage pupils when they have the right answer. They may be better placed to see if a pupil has pointed correctly and can often read the signs for the teacher and ensure the pupil is included in the oral session. If the class is chanting numbers to 10 the assistant may be tapping a pupil so as to reinforce the rhythm, or placing items one by one on the pupil's lap, to reinforce the learning.

The main role of the classroom assistant is to facilitate the inclusion of all pupils within the class. There is no reason why a classroom assistant should not take a small group for the oral mental session while the teacher takes the rest of the class if that will facilitate pupils participating in the session. It is important however that this is not always the same group, so that the teacher can also monitor and assess pupils' progress in this session. This is most likely to be helpful for pupils with severe communication difficulties where they will find it difficult to respond quickly to the teacher's questions and this might slow the pace of the lesson for everyone. It may also be useful for pupils with emotional and behavioural difficulties where they find it difficult to concentrate in whole-class sessions.

> **4. How can we organise and plan for mixed age classes?**

Special classes in mainstream and special schools often include quite a wide age range of pupils and age is often only one of the key factors in planning. The main challenges relate to prior attainment and the wide spread of learning objectives that have to be planned for. However, it is very important to consider age appropriateness. Often resources that are suitably motivating for certain age groups are not available to buy and many resources have to be made by teachers themselves. However, some resources are age neutral, e.g. number lines, digit cards, dice, and it is helpful for the mathematics coordinator to hold a good range of these. There are many number rhymes in the Appendix of this book and some of these are suitable for older pupils.

Teachers can choose objectives from the year group, based on pupils' abilities, to enable all pupils to benefit from the NNS. However, care needs to be taken that expectations of what pupils can achieve are sufficiently high and pupils are not taught lower level objectives because they are not expected to be able to achieve certain standards. Careful assessment and monitoring is clearly essential to ensure this is avoided.

> **6. How should we use ICT to support learning mathematics?**

Information and communication technology (ICT) has a particularly important role in both enabling pupils to access the lesson and to support the development of skills. Some pupils rely on ICT to communicate their understanding. Answers may need to be pre-programmed into talkers, Big Macs need answers programmed which change daily.

Data projectors linked to the class computer can be a very good way of using software to demonstrate a teaching point. This is a particularly useful tool for older pupils working on materials normally covered at a much younger age. The use of projector and screen has the effect of making the lesson more 'grown up'. It is also appropriate during the main activity for a pupil to use the computer for activities which support the learning objectives. This can be particularly appropriate where the pupil has profound learning difficulties and it is an integral part of their IEP.

Care needs to be taken not to use ICT just because it is there. It should be selected if it is the most efficient teaching method. It can be time consuming to set up and the software is often not as effective at making the teaching point as other methods would be. Section 2, page 31, of the NNS gives many ideas about how ICT can be used to develop mathematical skills and language and further software is regularly being developed.

> ### 7. How should we assess and record pupils' progress?

In addition to the regular daily informal assessment of pupils' progress, the NNS recommends two teaching sessions be allocated each half term to assess and record pupils' progress. They recommend the use of a class record sheet that lists the objectives taught over the half term which allows the teacher to mark the pupils who have attained the objectives. An example of this is in Section 2, on page 35, of the NNS Framework for Teaching Mathematics. However it may be easier to keep individual pupil records in cases where each pupil is working at a different level.

The following example shows a pupil who is largely working on P5 objectives with some at P6. The example is followed by a blank form which can be copied for use.

Individual Pupil Assessment Sheet

Name:	Level: P5	Half term: Autumn 2
Objectives taught:	Notes:	
Join in with familiar number rhymes, songs, stories and finger games either by body movement or vocalisation. Show recognition of the number names 1, 2, 3, 4 and 5.		
Join in with counting activities to 5, touching or pointing to objects with minimum support. Give just one number name to each object.		
Demonstrate an understanding of the concept of more/less and greater/smaller. Indicate which is more/less or greater/smaller when comparing the numerals 1 and 2 or a collection of 1 and 2 objects, using amounts up to 5.		

Individual Pupil Assessment Sheet

Name:	Level:	Half term:
Objectives taught:	Notes:	

8.   How do IEPs fit in to the planning?

It is important to assess the level of each pupil in order to plan appropriate IEP targets and to ensure progress.

An advantage in doing the Individual Pupil Assessment Sheets is that they can be appended to a pupil's IEP. They will provide evidence of clear targets and effective monitoring.

Group targets can be set for each small group that can become part of each pupil's specific IEP. IEP targets may also track back to earlier stages of the overall group or class target to ensure those pupils develop understanding of mathematical concepts. Extra small steps for certain pupils as recommended in the NNS may be introduced to simplify the content of the lesson, and to enable progress to be measured over time. Pupils benefit from practical mathematical activities and more emphasis is now placed on oral and mental activities, as well as practical explorations, and less on written evidence and instructions. Enlarged print, simplified instructions, additional support, pre-programmed communication aids and practical equipment can support achievement. Pupils' particular individual needs to access the daily mathematics lesson may be included in their IEP.

9.   How can we include all pupils in the daily mathematics lesson?

Why we need to include all pupils in the daily mathematics lesson

Pupils with a wide range of different special needs benefit from working alongside their peers in the daily mathematics lesson. The structure and routines of the lesson help provide security and predictability which all pupils with special needs value. It allows opportunities for pupils to learn from each other.

Including pupils who are anxious about learning mathematics

These pupils need concrete real life examples to relate to, which help develop their mathematical thinking. Problems need to be located in a setting which pupils can relate to. This will help pupils see the relevance of the mathematics and make connections to help them use and apply their new skills and knowledge. These pupils benefit from using real life resources like pictures of objects in their home or school and real money. They learn from role play and by physically experiencing what they need to learn. For example, they learn the value of money when using money to shop with rather than just looking at the coins. This is particularly important when developing work on measurements. Pupils need to understand the purpose of the activity. Is it clear to what purpose they are measuring, for example?

Including pupils who have problems with spatial awareness

These pupils may have problems in describing and understanding position, direction and movement. They need to be involved physically with their learning. When counting they need to physically move the objects or themselves. They might use a large number line on the floor and move as the counter. With these pupils teachers need to make mathematics a physical experience.

Including pupils who have problems with linguistic understanding

These pupils need to access the learning through using signs and symbols. They need to be used consistently throughout the school to reinforce their meaning. For example, the following might be the accepted symbol for the word 'pattern' and used throughout the whole school.

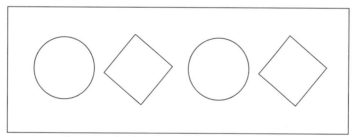

Many concepts can be taught by demonstration and need not rely on the use of spoken language. For example:

- a drum beat for demonstrating patterns;

- hold up digit cards to indicate that counting work is to be done.

In addition teachers need to find alternative ways for pupils to respond to questions and to share their understanding. They can do this by pointing to a number line that they have in front of them or showing digits cards. Some pupils have pre-programmed talkers which enable them to respond quickly to questions during a whole-class session.

Including pupils who have a challenging attitude towards mathematics

These pupils need to be engaged and motivated by the activities and resources used. Care needs to be taken to find the right level of challenge. Work that is too hard could easily make the pupil loose confidence but work that is too easy reinforces their already low view of their abilities in mathematics. Pupils who are a long way behind need age-appropriate activities to ensure that their self-esteem is boosted.

Including pupils who have visual and auditory difficulties

There are likely to be pupils in any class who learn best through either auditory or visual methods. It is important to provide a wide range of opportunities in lessons to address both methods. So when explaining a new piece of work ensure that there are visual clues to help these pupils. Present new concepts in an orderly visual form. It is important the numbers on a page are presented clearly in a sensible order.

4° Using questions

Why is questioning important?

Questioning is important because it:

- shapes thinking;

- promotes mathematical thinking;

- enables pupils to make choices;

- encourages communication;

- helps to develop mathematical understanding.

The NNS provides guidance for teachers on a wide range of questions that develop pupils' mathematical thinking. This is produced in a booklet called *Mathematical Vocabulary* published with the NNF. Many of these questions may be useful but they need adapting for pupils with learning difficulties as they are pitched at too high a level. This next section provides help in formulating good questions for different purposes.

Key questions to promote mathematical thinking

> **Show me an example of . . .**

A number
A square
A cube
A ball
A brick
A number 8
A number bigger than 3

A mathematical pattern
Something longer than this pencil
Something heavier than this box
Something on your left
Something in front of you
Something on/under the table
A time in the afternoon
A coin more than 1p

**After making a
choice: Why is it . . .**

A square?
A mathematical pattern?
A number smaller than 3?

**Tell me
something about . . .**

This mathematical pattern
This triangle
This box/cube
This coin

**Show or tell me
how to . . .**

Make a total of 3
Find the number that is 1 more than 2
Make a mathematical pattern
Find a bottle which holds more than this one
Find out how many teddies I have altogether
Find one more than 4
Make 5p with these coins
Find out what time it is

> **What do you think this problem is asking?**

When given problems about money, time, mass, length, capacity, addition, subtraction

> **What is the same and what is different about . . .**

A square and a triangle?
A circle and a sphere?
Two similar patterns?
Two clocks showing different times?
A 1p coin and a 2p coin?

> **This is a . . . . . .**
> **What else is it like?**

This is a blue square.
(Provide choice of square, blue things, things with 4 sides)

This is a 2p coin.
(Provide choice of bronze coins, coins more than 1p, etc.)

Questions at different levels

Some questions are easier to answer than others as they require a lower level of thinking. These types of questions include those that focus on recalling facts and applying facts. More difficult questions involve the respondent in hypothesising, predicting, comparing, interpreting and applying reasoning.

Examples of questions that involve recalling facts

What is 1 more than 3?

What is 2 add 1?

What number follows 3?

How many days a week do you come to school?

How many days in a week altogether?

How many fingers do you have?

What is the symbol for the number called zero?

How old are you?

What is your telephone number?

What date is your birthday?

Examples of questions that involve applying facts

If there are 8 children here, how many dinners do we need?

If there are 6 of us and we all have 1 biscuit, how many do we have altogether?

Give me two numbers that add up to 4.

There are 5 of us going swimming. How many wheelchairs will there be in the bus?

Examples of questions that involve hypothesising or predicting

How many marbles do you think there are in the jar?

Estimate how much you think this pint of milk will cost?

How long will it take us to walk to the shops?

How many squares can you see in the picture?

Which box do you think is bigger?

Which snake is longer?

What will happen if I push this tower of bricks?

What is the next shape in the pattern?

Examples of questions that involve designing and comparing procedures

How could we sort the colours of the bean bag?

How could we find out how many children are here today?

How could I share this apple between two people?

How could we find out how many drinks we need today?

Does this jar have more water in it than this one?

How could we find out if this box is bigger than that one?

How could we find out how many objects there are in the bag?

How can we find the length of this pencil? Are there other ways of doing it?

Examples of questions that involve interpreting results

What does this graph/picture/chart tell us?

Why has this side of the balance scales gone down?

After comparing 2 lengths: which is the longer?

After comparing 2 capacities: which holds more?

After comparing 2 masses: which is the heavier?

After comparing 2 numbers: which is the bigger?

Examples of questions that involve applying reasoning

We want to find out how many balls are in this bag. What should we do first? What shall we do next? And then what?

We want to find out who has the longest arm, which box is heavier, how many pencils in the jar . . . What should we do first? What shall we do next? And then what?

Examples of closed questions

Some pupils with more complex needs often respond better to closed questions:

Can you look at the toys?

Can you touch the toy?

Can you give me a toy?

How many bricks/cubes/toys are there?

Can you give me 3 bricks/cubes/toys?

What is 1p and 2p altogether?

Sweets cost 1p each. How much altogether? (give 4 sweets)

What is this shape called?

What is 6 add 1?

How many 2p cakes can you buy with 4p?

Examples of open questions

For more able pupils these questions promote, challenge and encourage thinking skills.

You have a bag of ones and a bag of threes. What numbers can you make? What numbers can you not make?

How many ways can you put 2/3/5 bricks on the table?

How can you make 10p using different coins?

Can you show me 3 different shapes and name them?

Give me a number bigger than 6.

Other questions that can help to extend children's thinking during a mathematics lesson

Children who are getting started with a piece of work

What do you need to get so that you can start?

Have you got everything you need?

Where are you going to begin?

What are you trying to do?

Which page will you start on?

Where will you start on the page?

Have you thought about how you are going to do this?

What help do you need?

Making positive intervention to check progress

Can you look at one like this?

Can you find one like this?

Can you tell me what you have put here?

Can you find the number 2/3/4 on the number line?

What are you going to do next?

Can you see a pattern?

Children who are stuck – or who need additional help

Why not make a guess and see if it works?

How can I help?

Look at mine.

Can you see my number?

Shall we try it this way?

Can you do this like me?

During the plenary

What did you find out about today?

What have we learnt about today?

Can you tell us how you did that?

How did we work out what to do?

Can you show us what you have done today?

What do you think you could do in the next lesson?

5 The learning objectives

This chapter contains the breakdown of the 11 key objectives for reception from the National Numeracy Framework. The objectives are consistent with both the P levels (QCA) and the latest publication from the DfEE which adds a Supplement of Examples for special schols (pupils working below level 1).

Strand 1: Numbers and the number system

Key objective 1: Say and use the number names in order in familiar contexts

Pupils will be able to:

P Level	Objective
P1	Begin to show a sensory awareness in relation to number rhymes, songs, stories and finger games using numbers.
P2	Respond through body movements or vocalisation to number rhymes, songs, stories and finger games using numbers.
P3	Show anticipation of the familiar number rhymes.
P4	Show an interest in number rhymes, songs, stories and finger games.
P5	Join in with familiar number rhymes, songs, stories and finger games either by body movement or vocalisation. Show recognition of the number names 1, 2.
P6	Join in with new number rhymes, songs, stories and games. Use numbers to 5 in familiar activities and games. Know the order of numbers to 5. Communicate number names to 5 in order.
P7	Use numbers to 10 in familiar contexts and games. Know the order of numbers to 10. Communicate number names to 5 in order.
P8	Use numbers beyond 10 in familiar contexts and games. Know the order of numbers to 20. Use ordinal numbers (first, second, third . . .) when describing positions of objects. Communicate number names to 20 in order. Recognise 'zero' in stories and number rhymes.

Strand 1: Numbers and the number system

Key objective 2: Count reliably up to 10 everyday objects

Pupils will be able to:

P Level	Objective
P1	Begin to show a sensory awareness of objects and counting activities which have an emphasis on one-to-one correspondence and object permanence.
P2	Respond through body movement or vocalisation to objects and counting activities in which one-to-one correspondence and object permanence is the key feature.
P3	Respond, with teacher help, to counting to 3 by touching or pointing once to each object. Show anticipation that when pointing to something it will be counted.
P4	Show an interest in counting activities. Show anticipation of pointing or touching objects and counting up to 2 at the same time.
P5	Join in with counting activities to 2, touching or pointing to objects with minimum support. Give just one number name to each object.
P6	Demonstrate their understanding of one-to-one correspondence. Join in rote counting to 5. Count reliably up to 3 objects. Demonstrate their understanding that the last number names the set.
P7	Join in rote counting to 10. Count reliably at least 5 objects.
P8	Join in with rote counting to numbers beyond 10. Continue the rote count onwards from a given small number. Count reliably at least 10 objects. Recognise a small number of objects without counting. Recognise 'none' when counting.

Strand 1: Numbers and the number system

Key objective 3: Recognise numerals 1 to 9

Pupils will be able to:

P Level	Objective
P1	Experience seeing and touching numerals 1, 2.
P2	Respond through body movements or vocalisation to feeling and touching activities involving the numerals 1, 2.
P3	Explore and manipulate cut outs of numerals 1 and 2.
P4	Show an interest in the numerals 1 and 2.
P5	Join in with identification of the numerals 1 and 2. Show some recognition of the numerals 1 and 2. Show understanding that each numeral is linked to a number name.
P6	Show some recognition of numerals to 5. Show understanding that each numeral has a constant shape. Show understanding that numerals can be used to record the number of objects.
P7	Make marks to record a number of objects they have counted. Reliably recognise numerals from 1 to 5.
P8	Recognise numerals from 0 to 9. Relate numerals to number of objects counted. Record numerals to represent up to 5 objects, with some reversals or inaccuracies.

Strand 1: Numbers and the number system

Key objective 4a: Use language such as more or less, greater or smaller, to compare two numbers

Pupils will be able to:

P Level	Objective
P1	Pupils at this level need to learn about these concepts in relation to
P2	real objects rather than in relation to numbers. These objectives are
P3	described in Strand 4 Key objective 4b (page 42).
P4	Show an interest in activities in which two numbers are being compared. Show recognition of the numbers being compared (1, 2).
P5	Join in with activities in which two numbers are being compared. Demonstrate understanding of the concept of comparison of two numbers.
P6	Demonstrate an understanding of the concept of more/less and greater/smaller. Indicate which is more/less or greater/smaller when comparing the numerals 1 and 2 or a collection of 1 and 2 objects, using numbers up to 5.
P7	Use mathematical language such as more or less, greater or smaller to compare given numbers of objects and say which is more or less using numbers up to 10.
P8	Compare two given numbers of objects saying which is more and which is less (or fewer) using numbers up to 10.

Strand 2: Calculations

Key objective 5: In practical activities and discussion, begin to use the vocabulary involved in adding and subtracting

Pupils will be able to:

P Level	Objective
P1	Experience through touching and seeing two objects being built and knocked down. Show reflex responses to sensory stimuli involving objects being put together and taken apart, and the words to describe these actions.
P2	Respond through body movements or vocalisation to activities where objects are put together (combined) and taken apart (partitioned). Respond to the word 'and', e.g. Jack *and* Jill.
P3	Respond to the words 'and', 'take away', when used in activities with objects that can be put together and taken apart.
P4	Show an interest in combining and partitioning activities and in the words associated with these activities. Show recognition of the operations of combining and partitioning.
P5	Join in with combining and partitioning activities. Show recognition of the words 'add', 'and', 'make', 'sum', 'total', 'altogether', 'take away'.
P6	Demonstrate their understanding of the concepts of combining and partitioning and of the words 'add', 'and', 'make', 'altogether', 'take away'.
P7	Use the language associated with combining and partitioning: 'add', 'and', 'make', 'altogether', 'take away'.
P8	When combining and partitioning objects, use the appropriate language to describe the activities: 'add', 'and', 'make', 'altogether', 'take away'.

Strand 2: Calculations

Key objective 6: In practical activities and discussion, find one more or less than a number from 1 to 10

Pupils will be able to:

P Level	Objective
P1	Pupils at this level need to learn about these concepts in relation to
P2	real objects rather than in relation to numbers. These objectives are
P3	described in Strand 4 Key objective 4b (page 42).
P4	Show an interest in activities of finding 1 more and 1 less than a 1 and 2. Show understanding of the words '1 more' and '1 less'.
P5	Join in with activities of finding 1 more and 1 less than a number 1 to 5.
P6	Demonstrate an understanding of the concepts 1 more and 1 less, using 1 to 5 familiar objects.
P7	Use '1 more' and '1 less' when finding 1 more and 1 less than 1 to 5 familiar objects. Find 1 more and 1 less than 1 to 5 objects.
P8	Find 1 more and 1 less than 1 to 10 objects and use the words 'more' and 'less' appropriately.

Strand 2: Calculations

Key objective 7: In practical activities and discussion, begin to relate addition to combining two groups of objects, and subtraction to 'taking away'

Pupils will be able to:

P Level	Objective
P1	At this level these objectives are the same as in Strand 2 Key objective 5 (page 37).
P2	
P3	
P4	Show an interest in combining and partitioning two groups of objects. Show anticipation of pointing or touching objects and counting the combined total of up to 3, or the number of items left after 1 or 2 have been taken away. Learn the words 'add together' and 'take away'.
P5	Join in with combining and partitioning activities, touching or pointing to the combined objects with minimum support. Show recognition of the words 'add' and 'take away'.
P6	Demonstrate their understanding of the concepts of combining and partitioning. Count reliably, up to 3, the total number of objects from the combining of two groups and the number of objects left in a group when 1 or 2 have been subtracted.
P7	Count reliably, up to at least 5, the total number of objects from the combining of two groups and the number of objects left in a group when some have been subtracted. Use the language associated with combining and partitioning: 'add', 'and', 'make', 'altogether', 'take away'.
P8	Count reliably, up to at least 10, the total number of objects from the combining of two groups and the number of objects left in a group when some have been subtracted. Use the language associated with combining and partitioning: 'add', 'and', 'make', 'altogether', 'take away'. Relate addition to combining two groups of objects and subtraction to taking away.

Strand 3: Solving problems

Key objective 8: Talk about, recognise and recreate simple patterns

Pupils will be able to:

P Level	Objective
P1	Experience simple mathematical patterns: for example, regular rhythms. Show an awareness of own objects and their permanence.
P2	Respond through body movement or vocalisation to activities involving the creation and continuation of simple mathematical patterns. Understand the concept of their own objects and begin to search for them using their eyes or bodies.
P3	Show anticipation of the next sound or object in a mathematical pattern. Explore and experience the objects used within mathematical patterns. Search and find own objects.
P4	Show an interest in creating and continuing simple mathematical patterns. Learn the sign, symbol, word for a mathematical pattern. Search and find missing familiar objects.
P5	Join in with the creation and continuation of simple mathematical patterns. Match, with help, objects and pictures.
P6	Demonstrate their understanding of the concept of a simple repeating mathematical pattern. Copy simple mathematical patterns.
P7	Recognise simple mathematical patterns. Talk about simple repeating patterns and attempt to recreate them.
P8	Talk about, describe, recognise, recreate and continue simple mathematical patterns.

Strand 3: Solving problems

Key objective 11: Use developing mathematical ideas and methods to solve practical problems

Pupils will be able to:

P Level	Objective
P1	Begin to show a sensory awareness of activities of practical 'real life' problems involving counting and comparing. Experience activities involving money. Show an awareness of own objects and their permanence.
P2	Respond through body movement or vocalisation to activities involving counting and comparing in 'real life' contexts and activities involving money. Understand own objects and begin to search for them using their eyes or hands.
P3	Respond appropriately to counting and comparing in 'real life' contexts and to coins. Search and find own objects.
P4	Show an interest in counting and comparing in 'real life' contexts and in coins. Show they understand that one action can cause another. Search and find missing familiar objects.
P5	Join in with activities involving counting and comparing in 'real life' contexts and with activities involving money.
P6	Use 1p coins in shopping for items up to 5p. Apply counting and comparing skills and knowledge to solve problems in 'real life' contexts.
P7	Use 1p and 2p coins in shopping for items up to 10p. Apply counting and comparing skills and knowledge to solve problems in 'real life' contexts. Begin to use mathematical ideas of matching and sorting to solve simple problems.
P8	Understand and use the vocabulary related to money. Sort coins and use them, in role play, to pay and give change. Apply counting and comparing skills and knowledge to solve problems in 'real life' contexts.

Strand 4: Measures, shape and space

Key objective 4b: Use language such as more or less, longer or shorter, heavier or lighter to compare two quantities

Pupils will be able to:

P Level	Objective
P1	Experience activities involving sequencing familiar events and the vocabulary of time. Explore objects that have different masses, lengths and capacities.
P2	Respond through body movements or vocalisation to activities involving the direct comparison of two lengths, two masses or two capacities and to those involving time.
P3	Show anticipation in response to the operation of directly comparing two lengths, two masses or two capacities and to the recognition of the operation of direct comparison.
P4	Show an interest in directly comparing two lengths, two masses or two capacities and to time-sequencing familiar events. Show recognition of the operation of direct comparison. Learn the signs/symbols/words for longer than/shorter than, shorter than/longer than, more/less.
P5	Compare one object with another according to its length or size responding to longer, shorter, bigger, smaller. Compare the timing of familiar events, responding to before, after, next, last.
P6	Demonstrate their understanding of the operation of comparing two lengths, two masses and two capacities. Show an understanding of vocabulary such as more or less when working with capacities. With support, they make a direct comparison of two masses. They compare the size of two objects and show awareness of the vocabulary larger than, smaller than.
P7	With support, they make direct comparison of two capacities. Use familiar words to describe size and quantity and time.
P8	Compare directly two lengths or two masses and find out by pouring which of two containers holds more or less. They show awareness of time through some familiarity with names of the days of the week and significant times in their day, such as meal times and bed times.

Strand 4: Measures, shape and space

Key objective 9: Use language such as circle or bigger to describe the shape and size of solids and flat shapes

Pupils will be able to:

P Level	Objective
P1	Experience the feel of 2D and 3D objects to develop the understanding of objects.
P2	Explore and respond through body movements or vocalisation to activities involving 2D shapes and 3D solids and develop their awareness of object permanence.
P3	Join in at appropriate times with activities involving 2D shapes and 3D solids. Show anticipation of 2D shapes and of 3D solids. Understand that different shapes have different names and they feel different.
P4	Show an interest in exploring the different properties of 2D shapes and 3D solids. Show recognition of circles, squares, cubes and spheres.
P5	Join in with activities involving naming 2D shapes and 3D solids. Match, with help, 2D shapes and 3D solids. Group or sort 2D shapes and 3D solids by attributes or properties of size or shape.
P6	Sort 2D shapes and 3D solids by attribute or property consistently. Show awareness of the names of 2D shapes and 3D solids. Learn the sign/symbols for straight and curved.
P7	Use some familiar words to name and describe the size of 2D shapes and 3D solids. Pick out particular shapes and solids from a collection. Describe familiar shapes and their attributes.
P8	Use mathematical vocabulary such as straight, circle, larger than to describe the shape and size of 2D shapes and 3D solids. Use a variety of 2D shapes and 3D solids to make and describe a simple model, pictures and mathematical patterns.

Strand 4: Measures, shape and space

Key objective 10: Use everyday words to describe position, direction and movement

Pupils will be able to:

P Level	Objective
P1	Experience activities involving position, direction and movement.
P2	Respond through body movements or vocalisation to activities involving position, direction and movement.
P3	Show anticipation of an item being **on** or **in** a particular place.
P4	Show an interest in activities describing position, direction and movement. Show recognition of positions, directions and movements. Begin to understand position and the relationship between objects, e.g. joining in with stacking or aligning objects. Learn the signs/symbols/words for 'in' and 'on'.
P5	Manipulate positions: stacking objects, lining them up, putting them in and out of containers. Join in with activities involving movement, and those describing position, direction and movement.
P6	Show understanding of words, signs or symbols that describe positions, directions and movements, over, under, left, right, up, down, forwards, backwards, sideways.
P7	Use some familiar words to describe position, direction and movement. They recognise forward and backwards directions.
P8	Use everyday words appropriately to describe direction, position and movement.

6 Suggested activities and resources for different age groups

This chapter together with Chapter 5 can be used as a basis for your own school's scheme of work. It contains ideas for activities and resources to meet the key objectives described previously.

Once the learning objectives for a class have been identified, numeracy coordinators may like to photocopy these pages adding in resources available in the school and additional activities that are appropraite to individual pupils or groups. Each activity has a box next to it and coordinators or teachers can tick the most appropriate activities for their class or age group.

There are four aspects to planning for each of the key learning objectives.

1. Mental oral work ideas (section A)
2. Main activities (section B)
3. Resources (section C)
4. Audit of our own school's activities and resources (section D)

There is a page for each of these to enable easy photocopying.

A Mental oral work ideas
Describes a range of activities to promote each objective in the first 10 minutes of the lesson.

B Main activity ideas
Describes activities that may be used to support the teaching in the main part of the lesson.

C Resources
Lists the resources that pilot schools have found useful.

D Audit of our own school's activities and resources
Should be used to list the school's own available resources together with the activities which work best for their classes.

Strand 1: Numbers and the number system

Key objective 1: Say and use the number names in order in familiar contexts

(A) Mental oral work ideas

- Whole-class number rhymes and games such as '1, 2, 3, 4, 5 once I caught a fish alive', '1 potato, 2 potato, 3 potato, 4', '5 little speckled frogs' (see additional rhymes in Appendices 1 and 2).

- Involvement in counting activities such as rote counting: counting numbers of pupils in class, numbers of boys/girls.

- Counting on and back from a given number to 10, then 20.

- Whole-class counting/reciting to a given number, e.g. 1, 2, 3.

- Whole-class counting in 2's, 5's (more able).

- Lower attaining pupils, e.g. PMLD pupils, can be involved in multi-sensory experiences of counting such as using musical instruments to beat the rhythm 1, 2, 3 as counting takes place. Rhythm can be tapped onto their shoulders/hands by adult or higher attaining pupils. They can be physically moved in wheelchairs, or by the hand, to be fully involved in number games.

- Whole-class recognition of mistakes as adult counts 1, 2, 4, 5.

- Listening to counting rhymes on tape and joining in.

- Watching familiar puppet or animated video number songs.

- Use of large puppet (preferably one that can sign) to help pupils stay on task; count by rote with the puppet.

- Clapping rhymes (see Appendix).

- Rap rhymes (see Appendix).

- Number stories (see Appendix).

- Numbers on: birthday cards, house doors, horses in a horse race, etc, to enable understanding that 'things have labels'.

- Pupils with severe complex or challenging behaviour, or autism, may undertake all of these activities, but might do so individually as part of their 'box work'.

Key objective 1: Say and use the number names in order in familiar contexts

(B) Main activities

Working with an adult in a small group or individually pupils can be involved in any of the mental oral activities for longer periods, concentrating on particular aspects. The following ideas expand on those activities.

- Use their fingers to count to 3, 5, 10.

- Use their fingers to count on from a given number, and back from a given number.

- Eye point, use a communication board, or point as they count to 3, 5, 10, or on from a given number, or back from a given number.

- Listen to number rhymes on tape as they explore objects, e.g. 5 little ducks, as they play with 3D ducks matched to the song, or 5 fat sausages, or 5 (plastic) green bottles.

- Use puppets to encourage joining in at appropriate level with counting activities as they count with rhymes, rap rhymes or songs.

- Adult arranges groups of objects in different ways. Pupils count with teacher to foster understanding that 1 is always 1; 2 is always 2, and always follows 1; 3 is always 3, and always follows 2. This will also foster understanding of labels, e.g. 3 is always 3 and *never* changes.

- Large number line on which pupils can jump/hop/be wheeled. Pupils actively count along the line as they take part in the game. This could be done in hall/playground/corridor.

- Counting pupils in class by rote.

- Counting how many pupils want dinner today.

- Counting boys/girls, by rote.

Key objective 1: Say and use the number names in order in familiar contexts

(C) Resources

- Range of number rhymes and games (see Appendix 1).

- Range of musical instruments.

- Puppets.

- Range of communication aids.

- 3D ducks, frogs, sausages.

- Stories which involve use of number, e.g. 3 pigs, 3 bears, 3 billy goats.

- Number lines of varying sizes.

- Range of objects to count that are age appropriate.

Tactile frogs help this group of pupils in activities relating to number on the theme of 5 speckled frogs.

Key objective 1: Say and use the number names in order in familiar contexts

(D) Audit of our school activities and resources

Activities we already use:

☐

☐

☐

☐

☐

☐

Resources:

☐

☐

☐

☐

Strand 1: Numbers and the number system

Key objective 2: Count reliably up to 10 everyday objects

(A) Mental oral work ideas

- Counting to 3, then 5, then 10 or 20 objects, or pupils, touching each one in turn.

- Whole-class games in which pupils are asked 'how many objects can you see here?' They count touching each in turn.

- Counting objects in a line such as, 10 green bottles, 5 little frogs (real objects).

- Counting objects on a washing line.

- Work with a different number for a week, i.e. count 2 objects (pens, bricks, button, teddies, bottles) and make a collection over the week of '2'. Display in the classroom.

- Explore objects, e.g. What's this? It's a ball.

- How many balls?

- How many pupils are here today?

- How many boys? How many girls?

- Use a tactile object with different textures, for example, soft as well as hard objects (plastic bears, soft balls, bricks).

- Build a train with bricks and count the carriages together.

- Build a road and count the cars.

- Higher attaining pupils can count on from a given number, and back from a given number.

- Count shopping items, e.g. cups, in appropriate contexts.

- Pupils who find it difficult to be part of a large group could undertake their mental/oral counting on a one-to-one basis, e.g. pupils with severe challenging behaviour or autism may take part in all activities on an individual basis.

Key objective 2: Count reliably up to 10 everyday objects

(B) Main activities

- Pupils have 5 dogs or cats, or hens made of card. They have to give each dog a bone, or each cat a mouse, or each hen an egg, ensuring there is one to one correspondence.

- Play small group games in which they take turns to count and touch objects to 3, 5, 10. Emphasise the last number said names the set.

- Use a simple number line/track to 3, 5, 10 and count together.

- Find how many shoes, trousers, jumpers they are wearing.

- Lower attaining/PMLD pupils can be encouraged to explore objects with a range of tactile experiences such as exploring with their hands in sand/jelly/pasta/water/to find an object.

- Lower attaining pupils can experience counting rhymes through listening to tapes (Objective 1) and counting the objects that match – with adult or more able pupils' help, i.e. 3 ducks, etc.

- Higher attainers can begin building their own number track using bricks or counting them.

- Simple threading activities in which pupils thread 3, 5, 10 beads, then count them.

- Build a tower of 5.

- Follow a snake pattern on the floor walking in the sections and counting as they go 1 2 3 4 5 6 7 making sure they put one step into each section. Working in pairs or small groups they take turns.

- In PE or in the hall, they do 2 jumps, 2 hops, touch 2 balls, 2 hoops, find 2 bean bags, etc.

- Posting letters: pupils post letters with correct numbers on envelope through matching door (with same number on it).

Key objective 2: Count reliably up to 10 everyday objects

(C) Resources

- Objects to count: washing line; coats; food basket; cups, bottles, etc.

- Number puzzles.

- Skittles games, dice games.

- Scoring games/board games.

- Turn-taking games.

- Number rhymes.

- Sets of toys, e.g. 3 bears, 3 pigs, 3 cups, 3 plates, etc.

- Number stores such as 3 bears, 3 pigs, 3 Billy Goats Gruff.

- Number lines in playground.

- Job rotas.

- Number games such as Snakes and Ladders.

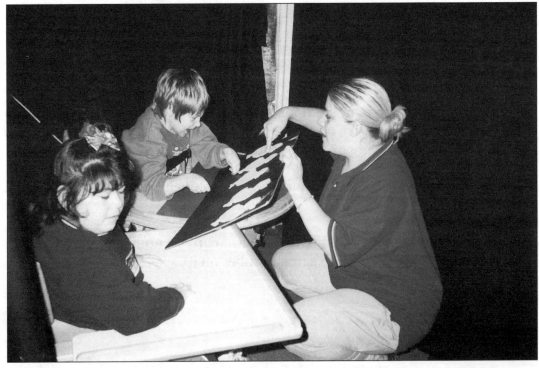

Pupils with visual impairment benefit from working in the dark room as part of their numeracy time. They look and join in with counting to 5.

- Number games such as a board with 5 dogs, cats or hens on it.

- Sensory resources to enable pupils to develop their understanding of how objects feel, such as work in the dark room related to object recognition and object permanence.

- Feely bag resources and activities in which pupils are encouraged to feel tactile objects.

- Sand, water, jelly or pasta resources to enable exploration and searching for objects, and to support the development of object permanence.

Key objective 2: Count reliably up to 10 everyday objects

(D) Audit of our school activities and resources

Activities we already use:

☐

☐

☐

☐

☐

Resources:

☐

☐

☐

☐

Strand 1: Numbers and the number system

Key objective 3: Recognise numerals 1 to 9

(A) Mental oral work ideas

- Whole-class games in which pupils identify by touching, eye pointing, signing, the numerals 1, 2, 3 and on to 5, 10 and 20.

- Number games such as 5 little frogs, 10 green bottles in which numerals can be used as labels.

- Whole-class games in which pupils are asked 'how many objects?' They count and label with a numeral.

- Pupils are given a means of communicating their answer. Either a communication aid, such as a talker, or switch; or a card on which numbers are printed appropriately. For lower attainers tactile numbers 1 to 3 may be appropriate. For others cards such as 1 to 9   1 to 3   0 to 3   may be appropriate.

  They should be fixed to their tray or table, or on the floor, depending on grouping. Pupils are then asked to point to, eye point, or indicate numbers as appropriate.

- Number stories and rhymes appropriate to age in which pupils can find and point to the numbers in the story, e.g. 3 Billy Goats Gruff, 10 Green Bottles.

- Washing line across the classroom. Pupils have individual numbers on trays/tables. They indicate 'which number comes next?'

Pupils are asked to identify a circle like the one on the board. Each pupil has their answer card appropriate to their needs to ensure all pupils can participate by pointing, eye pointing or touching the correct shape. Some pupils have the support of an intervener to enable their contributions to be seen and heard.

Key objective 3: Recognise numerals 1 to 9

(B) Main activities

- Identify their own age, birthday, house number – find number to label.

- More able pupils can play games such as Number Snap, i.e. find one the same, find all the '2's', find all the '5's?', etc. They can find the missing numeral in a line 1, 2, 3, 4, 6, 7, 8. They can complete simple number puzzles in a sequence.

- Lower attaining pupils can explore the shapes of numerals using cut out wooden shapes. They can explore objects which have the numeral attached, e.g. a teddy with a number 1 on. Pupils with PMLD can explore with their hands in sand/water/dough/jelly to find numerals. They can listen to taped rhymes and number stories. They can practise 'looking' at objects in the dark room: 'where's the ball?' (Use UV light where necessary.)

- Match numbers on cards to a given number line: 1–3, then 1–5, then 1–10, then 0–10.

- Dot-to-dot activities in which pupils try to guess which number will be revealed.

- Number games using dice, such as Snakes and Ladders, in which pupils use dice with 1–3 on, then 1–6.

Key objective 3: Recognise numerals 1 to 9

(C) Resources

- Large tactile numbers.

- Small tactile numbers.

- Large dice – some with restricted numbers such as 1 and 2 only.

- Numerals to hold up, peg up, stick to magnetic board.

- Wooden cut out numerals.

- Sand tray.

- Plasticine, dough.

- Number line.

- Cards with numbers on to enable sequencing.

- Number cards.

- Board games.

Key objective 3: Recognise numerals 1 to 9

(D) Audit of our school activities and resources

Activities we already use:

☐

☐

☐

☐

☐

Resources:

☐

☐

☐

☐

Strand 1: Numbers and the number system

Key objective 4a: Use language such as more or less, greater or smaller, to compare two numbers

(A) Mental oral work ideas

- Whole-class activities in which pupils watch/listen and respond as teacher holds up two numbers. Pupils point to, or indicate, which is greater than/more than the other – older pupils could use money, or shopping activities.

- Explore the concept of more/less, greater than/smaller than, etc., in relation to numbers on a number line. Which one is greater than the other?

- Whole-class discussion about how many pupils are in class. Is it more than or less than yesterday? Are there more boys? How many dinners do we need? 7, is that more than 6? Is it more than 9?

- How many cups do we need for 8 pupils? Is that more than 7? Is it more than 2?

- Teacher holds up fingers (2, 3, 4, etc.). Pupils asked to indicate more than 2, more than 3, more than 4. They can hold up fingers, point to numbers on a card, eye point, or use a switch to find more/less or a number greater than nine.

- Two large ladybirds with velcro spots. Pupils actively stick spots on ladybirds – which one has more spots?

- Teacher holds up a digit card. Pupils have to hold up/indicate/point to a number greater than that number or less than that number.

- Teacher holds up a picture of 2 teddies/biscuits/houses, etc. Pupil has to indicate/point to a picture with more teddies/biscuits/houses.

Key objective 4a: Use language such as more or less, greater or smaller, to compare two numbers

(B) Main activities

- Pupils work with adults to build a tower. Can you make one bigger than mine? Are there more bricks in yours or mine? Who has fewer than me? Make yours smaller.

- Card number game. Pupils work with adult to play card games. They use numbers they can recognise, i.e. 1–3, or 1–5, or 1–10. They take turns to find/turnover a card. Which one is bigger? Which one is smaller. Is that more or less than this one?

- Threading game: pupils thread beads on strings. Who has more than me? Who has less than me? Pupils with more complex needs work with adult to understand the concept of more than/less than, greater than/smaller than.

- Fishing game – who has caught more fish than me?

- More able or higher attaining pupils might be encouraged to work with numbers to 20, e.g. find a number greater than 12, smaller than 8.

- Use a dice to throw a number bigger or smaller than mine (large colourful dice are best).

Key objective 4a: Use language such as more or less, greater or smaller, to compare two numbers

(C) Resources

- Variety of large tactile numbers.

- Variety of large numbers to hang on a washing line.

- Stories to encourage comparisons, Enormous Turnip, Three Bears, Three Billy Goats Gruff.

- Shopping game and 'real' shop set up with objects priced appropriately.

- Washing to hang on a washing line (made of card or material).

- Bricks.

- Range of large, colourful dice with appropriate numbers or dots, i.e. 1–3, 1–6, etc.

- Range of age appropriate resources and objects to count and match.

- Fishing game with magnetic fish and hooks.

Key objective 4a: Use language such as more or less, greater or smaller, to compare two numbers

(D) Audit of our school activities and resources

Activities we already use:

☐

☐

☐

☐

☐

Resources:

☐

☐

☐

☐

Strand 2: Calculations

Key objective 5: In practical activities and discussion, begin to use the vocabulary involved in adding and subtracting

(A) Mental oral work ideas

- Whole-class building of towers or tracks in which pupils 'add another' or 'take one away' – teacher introduces and uses vocabulary.

- Musical chairs – taking 1 chair away.

- Counting how many boys are here today, how many girls, how many all together.

- How many pupils are having dinner? How many are having a packed lunch? How many altogether?

- Whole-class game in which teacher shows 2 cubes in 1 hand, and 1 cube in the other. Pupils indicate how many altogether. They may need cards on their trays or tables to enable them to indicate, point to, or eye point to the correct answer.

- Teacher holds up 2 fingers. What happens if I take 1 away? Same activity can be done with cakes, sweets, cups, etc. As above, pupils need a means of communicating their answer.

- Use of real objects such as oranges which have a tactile feel. Pupils are shown 1 orange on one side of table, 1 orange on other. They understand that 1 is 1 and will always be 1. 'How many will I have if I put the oranges together?'

Key objective 5: In practical activities and discussion, begin to use the vocabulary involved in adding and subtracting

(B) Main activities

- Simple puzzles in which pupils add 1 more and then take the piece away. This might include building towers, putting rings onto a central stem, completing stacking set, and then taking it apart.

- Bus game: pupils play a practical game with chairs set up like a bus. 1 pupil gets on the bus and is going to? (perhaps the shops). Another pupil gets on – how many now? What happens if 1 gets off?

- Simple building tasks with bricks, Lego, Duplo, stickle bricks, in which pupils add bricks together, and then take them apart.

- Musical chairs.

- Large building bricks in hall or corridor in which pupils add 1 more, 2 more, etc.

- Making paper chains to hang up, adding more and more.

- Cooking activities in which pupils add more currants to make a whole cake.

- Practical activities in which pupils are joined together to make a circle – then pull apart also to make a long line – then pull apart.

- Activities in which 1 more is added or taken away, i.e. everyday classroom activities.

- Problem-solving activities such as how many cups do we need? What happens if 1 pupil is away. How many do I need now?

Key objective 5: In practical activities and discussion, begin to use the vocabulary involved in adding and subtracting

(C) Resources

- Building blocks and bricks of varying sizes to build and pull apart.

- Lego bricks, cubes, etc., to build and pull apart.

- Combining and pulling apart activities, e.g. making a chain.

- Jigsaw puzzles.

- Items which stack.

- Train tracks.

- Objects from everyday life.

Key objective 5: In practical activities and discussion, begin to use the vocabulary involved in adding and subtracting

(D) Audit of our school activities and resources

Activities we already use:

☐

☐

☐

☐

☐

Resources

☐

☐

☐

☐

Strand 2: Calculations

Key objective 6: In practical activities and discussion, find one more or less than a number from 1 to 10

(A) Mental oral work ideas

- Singing games such as 5 little frogs, 5 little ducks, 10 green bottles. Emphasis should be placed on the idea of adding 1 more, or taking 1 away to make 1 fewer.

- Teacher holds up a number of fingers – pupils count; teacher takes 1 away; pupils find the number by counting together. This could be undertaken with real objects or cards.

- Activities that include 3D objects from stories, e.g. 3 bears, how many bowls do I need. Teacher finds 2, how many more? Or teacher finds 4 bowls, how many less? This could be undertaken with dolls house furniture – matching people to chairs, beds, etc.; or to a garage – matching people or garages to cars.

- 10 green bottles on washing line, 'let's take 1 away – how many left?'. Pupils need a means to communicate their answer, e.g. board/card on table with numbers, or bottles, so that they can indicate correct answer.

- Numbers on a number line. Pupils count how many – 1, 2, 3. Teacher adds 1 more number. Pupils count 1, 2, 3, 4. Teacher takes one away, etc. This activity can be undertaken with a range of 2D pictures of an object such as currant buns, balls, cups, or with real objects.

- Pupils make a line. Teacher takes one away. They count how many are left.

Key objective 6: In practical activities and discussion, find one more or less than a number from 1 to 10

(B) Main activities

- Feely bag activities: pupils are encouraged to pull out an object and put it on the table. Each pupil adds 1 more. They count how many. Then they each put one object away – counting each time.

- Activities in which pupils find 1 more plate, cup, biscuit.

- Musical games in groups in which they use 3D resources to add, or take 1 away (e.g. 5 fat sausages).

- Building activities with cubes. Pupils make a tower, and are then asked to count how many. Add 1 more and count how many. They then take 1 away and again count how many.

- Work with coins. 4 coins in a row. How many do I have? Take 1 away, how many now? They could do this as a practical task, at the shop where they take 4p to spend and buy 1 item for 1p.

- Musical chairs – taking one away.

- Giving out pencils, books, biscuits – 1 more needed.

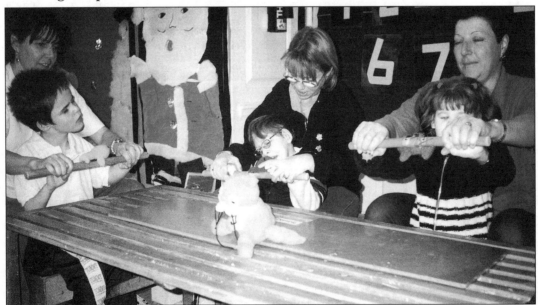

The teacher has incorporated the pupils' physio programmes with their mental oral part of the mathematics lesson. The pupils are moving their arms in time with the song 'Four little fish go swimming one day'. They grab and pull off their fish and feed it to the cat. The teacher reinforces the concept of 'take one away' through this activity.

Key objective 6: In practical activities and discussion, find one more or less than a number from 1 to 10

(C) Resources

- Cups and plates for activities in which 1 more is added such as 'add 1 more cup or plate'.

- Numbers on a line.

- Building blocks to add 1 more or take 1 away.

- Number rhymes/games such as 5 little ducks, frogs, currant buns.

- Coins, particularly 1p coins.

- Singing games in which they add or take away (e.g. 5 fat sausages).

- Range of real objects.

Pupils practice the number skills through playing board games

Key objective 6: In practical activities and discussion find one more or less than a number from 1 to 10

(D) Audit of our school activities and resources

Activities we already use:

☐

☐

☐

☐

☐

Resources:

☐

☐

☐

☐

Strand 2: Calculations

Key objective 7: In practical activities and discussion, begin to relate addition to combining two groups of objects, and subtraction to 'taking away'

(A) Mental oral work ideas

- Whole-class situation in which pupils have a means to communicate answers; either a switch talker or a number board with numbers or pictures as appropriate. They watch as the teacher puts 3 objects on one side of a table, and 2 objects on the other. They count 1, 2, 3 and 1, 2. The teacher puts the objects together and talks about combining them. Pupils count 1, 2, 3, 4, 5.

- This activity could be differentiated by using number cards on a washing line.

- Combining boys and girls. Boys sit in one area, girls in another. They count how many in each group. The two groups then combine, and pupils count again.

- Combining the group of pupils who have dinners, with those who have packed lunches.

- Teacher builds two towers with large bricks. Pupils watch as bricks are then combined. They count how many altogether. Teacher then takes some away to make another tower. Pupils count again.

- Show me 1 finger on 1 hand.
  Now show me 1 finger on the other hand.
  How many fingers altogether?
  Now put 1 away. How many left?

- Pupils with more profound difficulties at P1–3 will require adult support to build towers and knock them down to be aware of combining and taking apart (Objective 5).

Key objective 7: In practical activities and discussion, begin to relate addition to combining two groups of objects, and subtraction to 'taking away'

(B) Main activities

Range of activities for small groups in PE or in the hall or playground could include:

- Skittles game – how many have we knocked over? How many left?

- Number game – in hall; large numbers in each corner, i.e. 2, 1, 3, 1. Pupils then run to a corner and make sure that the right number of pupils are there. Teacher then asks two corners to combine, i.e. 2+1 or 3+1. How many now?

- Line game – pupils make lines one behind the other. Each line contains 2 or 3 pupils (maybe more for higher attainers). Teacher then asks each line to combine with another. How many altogether?

- Information and Communication Technology (ICT) – activities such as basic addition and subtraction tasks, e.g. Young Start.

- Acting out stories, i.e. using play – people going for a walk. 3 play together, 2 more come along – how many altogether?

- Spider game: pupils have a body; they add legs in 2s.

- Tray of cakes: pupils place cakes on two plates. They count each plateful. They then put them back into the cake tray – count again.

- Adding/taking away or spending coins as part of a shopping game, e.g. items cost differing amounts – 2p, 1p, 3p. Pupils buy 2 items – how much altogether?

- Objects in hoops: two hoops with range of different objects. Pupils put objects together and count. They then take some away and put them back in the other hoop.

Key objective 7: In practical activities and discussion, begin to relate addition to combining two groups of objects, and subtraction to 'taking away'

(C) Resources

- Number rhymes and songs.

- Plastic, magnetic numbers.

- Number line.

- Numerals.

- Range of real objects.

- Hoops.

- Skittles.

- Large blocks.

Key objective 7: In practical activities and discussion, begin to relate addition to combining two groups of objects, and subtraction to 'taking away'

(D) Audit of our school activities and resources

Activities we already use:

☐

☐

☐

☐

☐

Resources:

☐

☐

☐

☐

Strand 3: Solving problems

Key objective 8: Talk about, recognise and recreate simple patterns

(A) Mental oral work ideas

- Clapping rhythms, copying the teacher, e.g. clap hands, clap knees, clap hands, clap knees. Pupils at P1–3 may benefit from hearing an adult, or having a more able pupil to tap on their hands/knees for them.

- Making a pattern on the washing line. Teacher puts a circle and a square, or circle and a square. Pupils are asked to indicate on their answer boards what comes next.

- In PE, pupils recreate a simple pattern demonstrated by the teacher, e.g. arms up, arms down, arms up, arms down (pupils at P1–3 may require and benefit from adult help).

- Making patterns with pupils, e.g. 1 boy, 1 girl, 1 boy, 1 girl, 2 boys, 2 girls, 2 boys, 2 girls.

- Musical patterns – pupils have access to an instrument. They copy adult pattern – then initiate own. Use drum beats.

- Making patterns with everyday items such as plate, cup, spoon, plate, cup, spoon – pupils add on as appropriate.

- Identifying patterns in the classroom or the environment.

- Listening to repeating patterns in music, e.g. as in Peter and the Wolf.

Key objective 8: Talk about, recognise and recreate simple patterns

(B) Main activities

- Pupils use points to make a mathematical pattern, e.g. a cotton reel and a sponge repeatedly printed in a line.

- Cut out shapes such as □ ○ □ ○ □ ○. Pupils copy the pattern either by sticking or by using 3D resources.

- Tapping range of patterns on musical instruments.

- Threading beads in a mathematical pattern.

- Patterns in relation to physiotherapy exercises, e.g. arms stretch, arms down, arms stretch, arms down.

- In the playground or hall pupils can be encouraged to make patterns with bodies, e.g. hop, jump, hop, jump.

- Copying adult pattern with 3D shapes and continuing them.

Key objective 8: Talk about, recognise and recreate simple patterns

(C) Resources

- Collection of simple patterns, e.g. fabrics, wallpapers, wrapping papers from different cultures/traditions, music.

- Coloured beads and bricks.

- Counters.

- Musical clapping patterns, i.e. names, songs, rhymes, simple patterns.

- Printing materials, i.e. potato, blocks, bricks.

- Duplo bricks.

- Musical instruments.

Key objective 8: Talk about, recognise and recreate simple patterns

(D) Audit of our school activities and resources

Activities we already use:

☐

☐

☐

☐

☐

Resources:

☐

☐

☐

☐

Strand 3: Solving problems

Key objective 11: Use developing mathematical ideas and methods to solve practical problems

(A) Mental oral work ideas

Range of questioning tasks in which the teacher asks the group relevant mathematical questions, based on real life situations, making sure the group has the appropriate means of answering, e.g. number boards, shape boards, coins, communication aids. For example:

There are 10 pupils here today, how many dinners do we need?
If there are 4 boys and 6 girls, how many altogether?
How much will 2 apples cost if they are 6p each?
Can you give each pupil a biscuit?
Can you find one the same?
What number is missing?

See Chapter 4 'Using questions' for further ideas.

Key objective 11: Use developing mathematical ideas and methods to solve practical problems

(B) Main activities

- Pupils use a variety of equipment with which to gain understanding of mathematical concepts; for example:
Sand/water play – how many cups can we fill with this jug of water?;
building bricks – can you line up these bricks along the edge of the table?;
dough/clay – my house is 1 Dream Street. Make my house with its number.
Lining up and forming a queue – what pattern do we make if we line up this? Are there other patterns we can make?
Combining and partitioning activities – share these cakes out in the class. Are there any left?
Real shopping.
Pay for items, using change.
Cooking.
Measure out cake ingredients.
How many people fit in the bus?

Their ideas will develop depending on the questions asked and the way in which teachers structure the activities. See Chapter 4 'Using questions' for advice on this.

- Using developing mathematical concepts to support other subjects, e.g. measuring in Design and Technology, and in Science; position and direction in PE; patterns in Music and Art, data in Geography.

- Class shop
What can we buy for 3p?
How many different items can we buy for 10p?
Pupils go to the local shop to buy apples for lunch.
They need to decide:
  How many?
  What size?
  What colour?
They need to know:
  How many pupils?
  How much do the apples cost?
  How much money do they have?

Key objective 11: Use developing mathematical ideas and methods to solve practical problems

(C) Resources

- Range of mathematical games.

- Matching, threading, building, making resources.

- Clocks.

- Real money.

- Class shop.

- Sand/water trays and appropriate containers.

- Shapes 2D and 3D.

- Musical instruments.

- Number lines.

- Tactile numbers.

- Simple question cards.

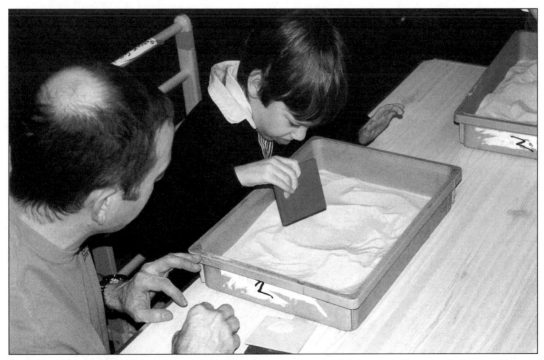

Pupils at the earliest levels of development enjoy exploring tactile media to find objects and develop their awareness of object permanence.

Key objective 11: Use developing mathematical ideas and methods to solve practical problems

(D) Audit of our school activities and resources

Activities we already use:

☐

☐

☐

☐

☐

Resources:

☐

☐

☐

☐

Strand 4: Measures, shape and space

Key objective 4b: Use language such as more or less, longer or shorter, heavier or lighter to compare two quantities

(A) Mental oral work ideas

- Practical games in which teacher demonstrates and pupils take turns to say which container holds more than the other or less than the other.

- Lining up in class: boys/girls – which line is longer than the other?

- Comparing heights of two pupils – who is taller, shorter than the other?

- Teacher holds up range of objects (comparing two), e.g. ribbons, string, rulers, balls, boxes. Pupils guess or estimate which is longer/shorter/heavier/ lighter than the other – using the language of comparison. They then check.

- Feel/touch the longer and shorter rope, heavy and light objects, small and large objects to gain understanding of heavy/big/long, etc., while the teacher is using the phrases 'this one is longer/shorter than that one', 'this one is heavier/lighter than that one', 'this one holds more than the other one'.

- Pupils with challenging behaviour may need to be introduced to the range of resources on a one-to-one basis or very gradually.

- Conkers or marbles in jars (two different quantities). Pupils asked to indicate which one holds more, which one holds less.

- Teacher builds two tracks. Pupils asked to indicate which one is longer, which one is shorter, than the other.

Key objective 4b: Use language such as more or less, longer or shorter, heavier or lighter to compare two quantities

(B) Main activities

- Working with sand/water tray. Pupils fill two containers, commenting on which container holds more than the other.

- Using a range of 3D resources, pupils identify which of two is shorter/longer snake, bigger/smaller box, heavier/lighter bricks, taller/shorter person.

- With pieces of string, pupils identify which are longer than the others, and which are shorter.

- Sorting 'like' objects into longer piles and shorter piles (or heavier/lighter, etc.).

- Building a track for cars or trains. Pupils asked to build two tracks, one longer than the other.

- Pupils build with bricks. They build a taller tower than the adult. They compare whose tower is taller than theirs.

- Compare shoes/coats, etc., within the group which ones are bigger?

- Compare 3D resources from stories, e.g. The Three Bears, Three Billy Goats Gruff, and The Enormous Turnip in differing stages of growth. Pupils look and comment on which is bigger than the others, which is smaller.

Key objective 4b: Use language such as more or less, longer or shorter, heavier or lighter to compare two quantities

(C) Resources

- Variety of everyday objects to compare (two of each).

- Sand and water tray with range of containers.

- Construction and model-making equipment to encourage comparing 'mine is bigger than yours'.

- Stories that encourage comparisons with multi-sensory props, e.g. Three Billy Goats Gruff.

- Comparing pupils' heights, shoe sizes.

- Range of objects such as snacks, boxes, solids, shapes, to enable comparisons.

- Range of balances and manoeuvres.

- Feathers, bricks, counters, house bricks, rulers, scales.

Key objective 4b: Use language such as more or less, longer or shorter, heavier or lighter to compare two quantities

(D) Audit or our school activities and resources

Activities we already use:

☐

☐

☐

☐

☐

Resources:

☐

☐

☐

☐

Strand 4: Measures, shape and space

Key objective 9: Use language such as circle or bigger to describe the shape and size of solids and flat shapes

(A) Mental oral work ideas

- Whole-class activity in which teacher asks pupils to look at shapes. Pupils have cards on desks/trays to enable answers to 'show me a circle' or 'show me the cube'.

- Teacher holds up range of circles and other 2D shapes. Pupils are taught 'this is a circle'/'this is not a circle'. They then identify on answer boards when a circle is held up. This is repeated as appropriate with other shapes.

- Shapes are on a washing line – 'show me the circle'.

- Squares on the washing line – 'show me the one that is bigger than all the others'.

- In PE, whole-class activity with shapes on the floor (big plastic ones if possible, or drawn chalk ones). Stand in a square, stand in a circle. Pupils in wheelchairs can be pushed to correct shape – if possible they should be asked to indicate 'is this the square?'.

- 'Let's all make a circle together' – physically move into a circle.
  'Let's make a square' – physically move into a square.
  'Arrange the chairs in a square/rectangle/triangle.'

- Circle games – 'Here we go round the Mulberry Bush', 'Farmer's in his den'.

- Guess the name of the shape or 3D object hidden under a cloth.

- Show a small part of a 2D shape above a screen. Pupils have to guess what shape it is.

Key objective 9: Use language such as circle or bigger to describe the shape and size of solids and flat shapes

(B) Main activities

- Each group finds range of shapes around the classroom and in the environment – 'Let's look for all the things that look like circles or have circles drawn on them'. Play 'find the rectangle' in the environment.

- Shape game in which the dice has shapes on it (restricted if necessary) and pupils throw the dice to obtain shapes to build a house or a person.

- Making stained glass windows in which pupils stick coloured shaped tissue onto appropriate cut out shapes.

- Make a collection of 3D solids for a solids table, e.g. tubes such as Smarties tubes, kitchen rolls, biscuit tubes, Rollos, label with 'cylinders'.

- Use shapes to create a shape boat, house or person as part of Design and Technology – solids.

- Build a model with bricks, copying the teacher and using appropriate shapes.

- Use sticky shapes to create a picture independently and be able to talk about the shapes used, using correct vocabulary.

- Make a collection of big circles or triangles, and fill a box or table with them. Then make a collection of small ones. Talk about differences. 'Find a bigger circle than mine.'

- Match shapes and objects and find one the same.

- Find shapes that match pre-prepared ones.

- 'Find all the squares in this tray, and put them in order of size.'

- Sorting games, e.g. sort out all the round buttons; sort out all the triangles; sort out all the Toblerone packets. Describe what they have in common.

- Explore with hands a range of 2D and 3D tactile shapes, using UV light or sensory room.

Key objective 9: Use language such as circle or bigger to describe the shape and size of solids and flat shapes

(C) Resources

- Range of 3D tactile media to feel and hold and explore.

- Junk modelling materials.

- Construction toys.

- Sticky shapes to create picture.

- Collections of shapes and solids.

- Large PE shapes.

- Answer boards and communication boards.

Key objective 9: Use language such as circle or bigger to describe the shape and size of solids and flat shapes

(D) Audit of our school activities and resources

Activities we already use:

Resource:

Strand 4: Measures, shape and space

Key objective 10: Use everyday words to describe position, direction and movement

(A) Mental oral work ideas

- Lining up in class: Who is first, second? Who is in front of Jack? Who is behind Lisa?

- In whole-class PE activities, pupils are asked to go under, or in, apparatus; or pupils are pushed to enable experience of position. Pupils describe position of others ('Simon is on the mat', 'Tom is under the box').

- Singing games such as 5 little frogs jumping 'in' the pool; '10 in the bed'. Use puppets to show the position.

- Range of activities in which teacher puts resources in / on / under next / to / behind / in front of other objects. Pupils discuss where the objects are.

- Stories that describe position, such as Three Billy Goats Gruff, as well as those described in the Numeracy Strategy, Section 4, page 27.

- Whole-group games, such as 'In and Out the Dusty Windows', and activities such as the conga or a snake in which pupils follow each other in, out, up, down, etc.

- Lining up or queueing for other lessons and dinner. Pupils are first, last, second, etc. 'Whose going to be first today?'

Key objective 10: Use everyday words to describe position, direction and movement

(B) Main activities

- Use of play people and soft toys as appropriate. Pupils play with toys and put them in different positions. They talk about it with adults, using appropriate vocabulary.

- Play house activities – putting things in the oven, on the oven, in the cupboard, in the bed, under the chair, etc.

- PE activities in which small groups or individuals work towards understanding of position by going 'in' boxes, 'under' benches, 'through' tunnels, etc.

- Treasure hunt activity in which pupils look in, on, under, behind, to find a particular reward.

- Play with cars and garages – putting the car on the ramp in the garage, over the bridge, etc.

- Farm animal play activities – cows in field, pigs in sty; and tractor in shed, milk in bucket, etc.

- Range of containers. Pupils put resources such as bricks, cubes, counters 'in' the containers. One container is upside down – they put counters 'under' that one.

Key objective 10: Use everyday words to describe position, direction and movement

(C) Resources

- Collections of objects and containers to put things in/on/under/beside.

- Language activities, and labels relating to position displayed around the classroom.

- Collections of objects such as teddies, cups, bricks.

- PE equipment.

Key objective 10: Use everyday words to describe position, direction and movement

(D) Audit of our school activities and resources

Activities we already use:

Resources:

Warm up mental maths ideas – overview

- Create a birthday train.
  Pupils draw picture of themselves/photo.
  Put it onto a carriage identifying month.
  'Who is in the first carriage, which month is your carriage in?'

- Number cards (large) for ages – pupils order themselves.
  Who is the oldest, youngest, less than, more than, the same?

- Recite number rhymes.

- Count number of children, how many here, how many away.

- Number line for school dinners.
  Number line for packed lunch.
  Number line for going home.

- Which is more than, less than:
  Number of boys/girls?
  Are there more boys than girls?
  Are there less boys than girls?
  What is the difference?

- Jumping Jacks.

- Teacher hides large number card – holds it up. Pupils shout answer.

- Frog on a track – where shall he land, they suggest and do.

- Simple number puzzles.

- Clock – recognition of numbers – identify o'clocks.

- Card game: pre-level R – recognition of objects, numerals 1, 2, 3.
  Level R – recognition of numbers to 10.
  Level 1 – recognition of number drawn 1–20.
  Level 2 – sum of two numbers drawn.
  Is this more or less than 5/10.
  Is this a bigger number than 5, etc.

- Numbers on birthday cards.

- Numbers on home doors.

- Bingo game.

- Counting number of pupils by touching each in turn. How many here today?

- Large tactile cut out digits for pupils to feel.

- Tactile singing rhymes with objects to put and take away, e.g. 5 little ducks.

- Singing number games and rhymes.

- How many hands, shoes, eyes, nose, ears, etc. have you got? touching each in turn.

- Passing 2D shapes and 3D solids around the group – each pupil is helped to feel and touch while teacher describes, using words like curve, straight, corners, edges.

- Recognition of colour – pupils experience a particular colour focus, e.g. everything red on the table today they touch, look, hold, while teacher says 'red'.

- 'Feely bag' with a range of objects of different textures – pupils say what they can feel.

- Birthday cake with real candles – count together.

- Finding, indicating, eye pointing, to 'own' cup, coat, shoes.

- Number stories.

7 Planning

The main Framework for Teaching Mathematics consists of yearly teaching programmes, or programmes of study summarising objectives for each year from Reception to Year 6 (see page 38 of the NNF). Each year contains certain Key objectives to which priority should be given within planning. The NNF offers guidance in respect of planning by offering planning grids for each yearly programme. These grids indicate the topics that should be taught and the recommended number of lessons for each topic (see Section 3 NNF). Mixed age classes are catered for within the planning as the grids for Y1 and Y2 and for Y3 and Y4 and for Y5 and Y6 correspond very closely.

The DfEE have now produced further guidance on planning numeracy for pupils with SLD and PMLD (January 2000). This guidance can be found in 'The Green Box – Professional Development Materials 3 and 4'. In the box is a spiral bound book called *Guidance for Your Professional Development: Book 4*.

In Chapter 7 – Addressing Special Needs in Mathematics Lessons, page 146 suggests that SLD and PMLD schools may wish to base their planning on the National Numeracy Framework planning grids:

YR 1 and 2, use the YR planning grid
Y3 and 4, use the Y1 planning grid
Y5 and 6, use the Y2 planning grid.

This advice can be applied if the class has pupils who are at level 1 even if there are some pupils working at much lower levels. This ensures that expectations are appropriate and earlier objectives can be inserted for the less able pupils. However where all the pupils are working below level 1, the YR planning grid can continue to be used for pupils in Y3 to Y6.

The examples on pages 147 and 148 of the DfEE guidance assume there are a number of pupils in the class across a wide ability range. Objectives can be selected from chapter 5 to insert in the planning grid, which match the pupils needs.

This frequent revisiting of topics over the terms is proving to support pupils with learning difficulties as well.

Pupils with SEN in mainstream schools are catered for within the NNF (see pages 18–23). The philosophy of the NNF is one of inclusion and teachers are encouraged to include all pupils with SEN in whole-class mathematics lessons wherever possible, with an emphasis on support and access, with appropriate adaptations. Pupils with more complex special needs may require individual learning programmes within the main body of the lesson. Their needs can be catered for in the 'whole-class' sessions by ensuring that the content is suitable for all pupils. Pupils' IEPs should be used to indicate modifications to the teaching programme, particularly in the main body of the lesson where they may receive additional support.

Principles of good planning

Long term plans: the Framework – what you will teach long-term over the year, i.e. which objectives from Chapter 5 are to be taught during the year.

In the long term plan for the year, the overall teaching programme for the class needs to be identified. This will include the appropriate year's outline from the NNS Famework for Teaching Mathematics. For pupils working towards level 1, the reception pages (pages 3–5 Section 3) should be used. The Key objectives can then be pasted in to the right hand column from Chapter 5 of this book depending on the ability levels within the class. Where there are some pupils working from later objectives they can be matched and pasted in on the same grid.

Medium term plans: Outline of the term's work – what you will cover and when (see example on page 99 and 100).

This provides the basis for short-term planning and should focus on which of the objectives or parts of the objectives will be taught across the term.

Procedures for devising medium-term plans for pupils with severe and profound learning difficulties should reflect the planning advice on page 41 of the NNF:

- common formats for planning a balanced programme of work should be developed;

- staffing/support allocations should be agreed;

- planning deadlines should be adhered to;

- monitoring and evaluation of planning and progression should be established.

The planning grid format suggested in Section 3 should be used.

Short term plans:
Short Term Plans: Lesson Weekly/Two weekly plans relating to tasks, questions, activities, grouping and staffing. [Example on pages 101–106]

Short-term planning can be on a daily, weekly or fortnightly basis, but common procedures should be established across the school.

Short-term planning is characterised by stating 'how' each topic or each objective will be taught, and by identifying resources, staffing and assessment opportunities.

Planning in the short term should take account of the following questions:

- How will I teach this?

- Which staff will be allocated to which pupil?

- What do I expect outcomes to be?

- How will I know that the pupils have made gains in knowledge?

- How much time will I allocate?

Example medium term plan

Mathematics
First Half Autumn Term
Every day 11.00–11.45

Number of sessions	Topic	Learning objectives Pupils will be taught to
5	Pattern (Objective 8)	– talk about, recognise and recreate simple patterns – have a given 'blob' and an add rule to make a pattern
5	Counting Comparing and Ordering (Objective 2)	– say the number names to 5 in familiar contexts – recite the number names in order 1–10 – use more/less to compare two numbers, or amounts where one number is smaller than the other
5	Shape and Space (Objective 10)	– use everyday words to describe position – put in order 3 objects with an evident difference in size
3	Addition and Subtraction (Objective 5)	– in practical activities and discussion, begin to use the vocabulary involved in adding and subtracting – understand combining and partitioning, e.g. putting things together and taking them apart
2	Addition and Subtraction (Objective 6)	– find one more, or one less, than a number up to 5
5	Measures (Objective 4)	– begin to use vocabulary of time, including before, after, next, later, earlier – talk about experiences, such as events in the day – sequence up to 3 familiar events
6	Measures (Objective 4)	– make direct comparisons of two masses, using language heavier than/lighter than – fill and empty containers, using language such as full/empty, holds more/less
3	Assess and Review	

Total 34 days

100

Example medium term plan

**Mathematics
Second Half Autumn Term
Every day 11.00–11.45**

Number of sessions	Topic	Learning objectives Pupils will be taught to
3	Number names (Objective 1)	– say and use the number names in order in familiar contexts – understand that things have labels (e.g. 2 is a label, and that numbers come in a particular order (e.g. 2 always follows 1)
5	Numerals (Objective 3)	– recognise numerals to 5 and understand each numeral has a constant shape – show understanding that each numeral is linked to a number name
5	Shape and Space (Objective 9)	– use language such as circle, triangle, square to describe 2D shapes – group and sort 2D shapes by properties (edges, corners)
5	Counting (Objective 2)	– count reliably up to 5 objects understand one-to-one correspondence – understand the twoness of 2
5	Capacity and Mass (Objective 4b)	– use of language: more than/less than to compare capacity of two containers – use of language: heavier than/lighter than to compare mass of two objects
2	Numbers (Objective 2)	– recognise none and zero in stories and rhymes
5	Addition and Subtraction (Objective 7)	– begin to relate addition to combining two groups of objects, and subtraction to partitioning – relate combining to groups of objects, e.g. 3 cups and 2 cups is 5 cups
3	Assess and Review	

Total 33 days

Examples of short term planning
Example Lesson Plan 1

Key objective: Talk about, recognise and recreate simple patterns

Specific objective: Pupils will be able to recognise, copy and recreate simple mathematical patterns

Mental oral session (10 minutes)
Ensure that all pupils are involved in the session, either by experiencing the beat through body taps or by joining in with clapping.

- Introduce clapping patterns (e.g. clap, clap, rest, clap, clap, rest, etc.).

- Use drum to beat out a pattern (e.g. short, short, short, long, short, short, short, long, etc.).

- Peg coloured cards to washing line (e.g. red, yellow, blue, green, red, yellow, blue, green, etc.).

- Peg digit cards to number line (e.g. 5, 2, 5, 2, 5, 2, 5, 2, etc.).

- Peg large coin cards on washing line (e.g. 1p, 10p, 50p, 1p, 10p, 50p, etc.).

- Use large boxes covered in different coloured wrapping paper, arrange in a pattern (e.g. boxes covered in silver, gold, silver, gold, etc.).

- Draw mathematical pattern on white board (e.g. || • || • || • || • || •).

Pupils experience the patterns. Teacher describes the pattern and asks for next one. Teacher introduces the word/symbol/sign for pattern.

Main activity (30 minutes)
Pupils are grouped by prior attainment

Squares
(P1–3) Working from own IEP targets. Working with LSAs to experience patterns using a variety of materials. Pupils to be encouraged to explore and experience the objects used in the pattern. For example, drum beat, body movements (arms out, arms in, arms out, arms in), selection of materials from above.

Triangles
(P4 & 5) Pupils given beads and string to thread to match patterns.
Pupils use blocks to copy patterns on cards.
Cards provided with pictures of simple mathematical patterns.

Circles
(P7 & 8) Pupils recreate patterns using a variety of materials – beads and threads – from pictures on display or patterns made by others.

Plenary (10 minutes)

Circles to show their patterns. They are passed around for pupils to explore and feel. Pupils asked what might come next. Others feel and touch patterns. Drum beat and clapping patterns to finish. All pupils to join in, with a Learning Support Assistant involved as necessary.

Key word: Pattern (to be displayed prominently in the classroom) together with lots of examples of mathematical patterns.

Example Lesson Plan 2

Key objective: Use language such as more or less, longer or shorter, heavier or lighter to compare two quantities

Specific objective: Pupils will be able to compare two masses and identify which one is heavier than the other

Mental oral session (10 minutes)
Each pupil is given two boxes to hold and explore – one is heavier than the other. Introduce the concept and vocabulary 'heavier than', 'lighter than' (words/symbols and signs). Pupils to hold heavier box, then lighter box. Repeat with two stones, two toys, two blocks, etc., each time teacher identifying the heavier item, then the lighter item. More able pupils asked to identify for themselves which is heavier/lighter than the other. (*Note.* Ensure items, in most cases, are the same size and same colour to avoid misconception.)

Main activity (30 minutes)
Pupils are grouped by prior attainment

Squares
(P1–3) Working from own IEP targets. Working with LSAs to experience and explore pairs of similar items, one which is heavier than the other. Pupils to be encouraged to explore and experience the objects used. They should hold one first, then the other. Then they should hold one object in each hand. Teacher/LSA to reinforce vocabulary: 'This is heavier than that', 'This is lighter than that'.

Triangles
(P4 & 5) Play with similar objects which have different masses. Take two and compare by feeling and exploring. With teacher direction, identify which one is heavier than the other. Choose another two and repeat, each time identifying which one is heavier/lighter than the other.

   Use a wide variety of items and ensure that, in several cases, pupils are comparing items which are the same in all attributes except their mass. Pupils match the label (written or sign or oral) 'heavier than', 'lighter than', with the appropriate item.

Circles
(P7 & 8) Pupils given pairs of items which have different masses. Asked to find out which is heavier than the other, and which is lighter than the other.

   Provided with a pan balance and shown how to use it. Pupils taught that the side that goes down farther than the other has the item in it which is heavier than the other. Pupils asked to find out, for each of their pairs of objects, which one is heavier than the other and which one is lighter. Pupils to put objects in pairs. All the heavier items should be placed on the left hand side and all the lighter items on the right hand side.

Plenary (10 minutes)
Pupils from the *circles* group to 'show and tell' others about the pan balance and demonstrate its use using two new items. Some items (e.g. blocks) are given to all pupils to feel and explore and compare for themselves. Teacher labels (written flash card, sign, orally) the heavier and lighter items.

At end of the lesson create an interactive table display of pairs of items identifying which one is heavier than the other, which one is lighter than the other. Display to include pan balance for use by pupils in unstructured time.

Key words: Heavier than, lighter than (to be displayed with items on table).

Example Lesson Plan 3

Key objective: Count reliably up to 10 everyday objects

Mental oral session (10 minutes)
Arrange three pupils at the front of the classroom, facing the rest of the group. Say 'today we are going to count how many pupils there are because we need to know how many dinners to order'. Count the three pupils ensuring that

- each pupil is touched as they are counted;

- the number name is said/signed as they are counted;

- the last number said is declared as the total.

Count them again, this time placing a large sign around their necks with the number written on, ensuring that the above points are again followed. Pupils return to their places. Pupils are given a number of items to count (these may be placed on their trays or in their laps).

Teacher/Learning Support Assistant (LSA) helps pupils count by touching/pointing to each item (differentiate for prior attainment).

Teacher holds up puppets at the front of the class and pupils count together focusing on pointing to each one as number is said/signed, and the last number said is the total count. Repeat with other items, e.g. soft toys, other pupils, bricks, pencils.

Main activity (30 minutes)
Pupils are grouped by prior attainment

Squares
(P1–3)   Working from own IEP targets. Working with LSAs to experience and explore one item, as the LSA says the word/signs 'one'. Then two items – the LSA touches the first and says/signs 'one' then passes the second item and says/signs 'two'. LSA says 'There are two . . .' Items to use, bricks/toys/pencils/cups/cards, etc.

Triangles
(P4 & 5) Pupils given two items (e.g bears/toys/pencils/bricks/cubes, etc.). Asked 'How many have you got?' With help, joins in touching/ pointing/eye pointing to each one in turn saying/signing with each 'one, two'. Pupil then says/signs 'I have two . . .'. Pupils given digit cards to hold up – teacher puts 1 or 2 items on their tray, pupils asked to hold up correct card to indicate how many items they have on their tray. Additionally pupils asked the following questions, and have to hold up digit card in response, or hold up correct number of fingers to say/sign number.

- How many arms have you got?

- Ears?

- Eyes?

- Noses?

- Legs?

- Mouths?

- Feet?

- Hands?

- Tummies?

Circles

(P7 & 8) Pupils shown a washing line. Teacher/LSA pegs a number of socks on the line. Pupils asked 'How many socks are on the line?' Pupils touch/point/eye point each in turn and identify correctly number of socks, then say/sign the answer. Other items are pegged on the line, e.g. jumpers, shorts, gloves, hats and other items of clothing. Increase number of items to stretch pupils' counting ability. Reinforce with digit cards.

Plenary (10 minutes)

String washing line across classroom so all pupils can see.

Peg on a few items. Pupils to count and hold up digit card to represent total.

Differentiate for triangles/squares/circles.

Key words: Count, one 1, two 2, three 3, etc. Have all displayed prominently around the classroom including on a number line.

Appendix 1: Traditional number rhymes

Two little eyes to look around
Two little ears to hear each sound
One little nose to smell what's sweet
One little mouth that likes to eat

One potato, 2 potatoes
3 potatoes, 4
5 potatoes, 6 potatoes
7 potatoes more

1, 2 buckle my shoe
3, 4 knock at the door
5, 6 pick up sticks
7, 8 lay them straight
9, 10 a big fat hen

When Goldilocks came to the house of the bears what did her 2 eyes see?
A bear that was big
A bear that was small
A bear that was middle sized, that was all she counted then 1, 2, 3

5 little ducks
5 little speckled frogs
5 little buns in the baker's shop
5 little monkeys
5 fat sausages
10 green bottles
10 in the bed

Addition to counting

Open the oven
It's very hot
Put in the loaves
In they pop
1 on the bottom
1 on the top
How many loaves altogether?

5 little peas
In a pea pod pressed
1 grew, 1 grew
and so did all the rest
they grew and grew
and did not stop
until the day
THE POD WENT POP

One, two, buckle my shoe

One, two, buckle my shoe
Three, four, knock at the door
Five, six, pick up sticks
Seven, eight, lay them straight
Nine, ten, a big fat hen

Eleven, twelve, dig and delve
Thirteen, fourteen, maids a courting
Fifteen, sixteen, maids in the kitchen
Seventeen, eighteen, maids in waiting
Nineteen, twenty, my plate's empty

One Little Speckled Frog

One little speckled frog
Sat on a speckled log
Eating some most delicious grubs
Yum Yum

One for the Money

One for the money
Two for the show
Three to get ready
And four to go

I Love Sixpence

I love sixpence, jolly jolly sixpence
I love sixpence as my life
I spent a penny of it, I spent a penny of it
I took fivepence home to my wife

I love fourpence, jolly jolly fourpence
I love fourpence as my life
I spent twopence of it, I spent twopence of it
I took twopence home to my wife

I love twopence, jolly jolly twopence
I love twopence as my life
I spent twopence of it, I spent twopence of it
I took nothing home to my wife

My Father Left Me

My father he left me just as he was able
One bowl, one bottle, one table
Two bowls, two bottles, two tables
Three bowls, three bottles, three tables
Four bowls, four bottles, four tables
Five bowls, five bottles, five tables
My father he left me just as he was able

Hot Cross Buns

Hot Cross Buns
Hot Cross Buns
One a penny, two a penny
Hot Cross Buns

If your daughters do not like them
Give them to your sons
One a penny, two a penny
Hot Cross Buns

Chook, Chook, Chook

Chook chook chook chook chook
Good morning Mrs Hen
How many chickens have you got?
Madam, I've got ten

Four of them are yellow
And four of them are brown
And two of them are speckled red
The nicest in the town

Magpies

I saw seven magpies in a tree
two for you, and five for me
One for sorrow, two for joy
three for a letter, four for a boy
Five for silver, six for gold
Seven for a secret never to be told

Jenny Wren

Jenny Wren last week was wed
And built her nest in Grandpa's bed
Look in next week and you will see
Two little eggs, and may be three

The Dove

The Dove says 'coo', 'coo' what shall I do?
I can scarce maintain two

Pooh, pooh says the wren
I've got ten
And keep them all like gentlemen

Three Blind Mice

Three blind mice
Three blind mice
See how they run
See how they run
They all run after the Farmer's wife
Who cut off their tails with a carving knife
Did you ever see such a thing in your life
As three blind mice?

Three Young Rats

Three young rats with black felt hats
Three young ducks with new straw flats
Three young dogs with curly tails
Three young cats with denim veils
Went out to walk with two young pigs
In satin vests and sorrel wigs
But suddenly it chanced to rain
And so they all went home again

As I was going to St Ives

As I was going to St Ives
I met a man with seven wives
Each wife had seven sacks
Each sack had seven cats
Each cat had seven kits
kits, cats, sacks, wives
How many were going to St Ives?

Five Little Pussy Cats

Five little pussy cats sitting in a row
Blue ribbons round each neck, fastened with a bow,
Hey pussies, Ho pussies, Are your faces clean?
Don't you know you're sitting there so as to be seen?

One Two Three Four Five

1, 2, 3, 4, 5
Once I caught a fish alive
6, 7, 8, 9, 10
Then I let him go again
Why did you let him go
Because he bit my finger so
Which finger did he bite?
This little finger on my right

I Saw Three Ships

I saw three ships come sailing by
come sailing by, come sailing by
I saw 3 ships come sailing by
On Christmas Day in the morning.

And what do you think was in them then
Was in them then, was in them then?
And what do you think was in them then
On Christmas Day in the morning?

Three pretty girls were in them then
Were in them then, were in them then
Three pretty girls were in them then
On Christmas Day in the morning

One could whistle, and one could sing
And one could play on the violin
Such joy was there at my Wedding
On Christmas Day in the morning

One Old Oxford Ox

1 old Oxford ox opening oysters
2 toads, totally tired, trying to trot to Tidsbury
3 thick thumping tigers taking toast for tea
4 finicky fishermen, fishing for finny fish
5 frippery Frenchmen foolishly fishing for frogs
6 sportsmen shooting snipe
7 Severn salmon swizzling shrimps
8 eminent Englishmen eagerly examining EUROPE
9 nimble noblemen nibbling nectarines
10 tinkering tinkers with 10 tin boxes
11 elephants elegantly equipped
12 top hats topically worn by top-hatted types

Mary at the Kitchen Door

1, 2, 3, 4
Mary at the kitchen door
5, 6, 7, 8
Eating cherries off a plate

Three Little Ghosts

Three little ghosts
Sitting on posts
Eating buttered toast
Greasing up their fists
Right up to their wrists
Oh what little beasts
To have such a feast

1, 2, 3

1, 2, 3
I love coffee
Billy loves Tea
How good it can be
1, 2, 3
I love coffee
And Billy loves tea

Five Little Speckled Frogs

Five little speckled frogs
Sat on a speckled log
Eating some most delicious bugs
Yum Yum
One jumped into the pool
Where it was nice and cool
then there were four green speckled frogs
Yum Yum

Four little speckled frogs
Sat on a speckled log
Eating some most delicious bugs
Yum Yum
One jumped into the pool
Where it was nice and cool
then there were three green speckled frogs
Yum Yum

Three little speckled frogs
Sat on a speckled log
Eating some most delicious bugs
Yum Yum
One jumped into the pool
Where it was nice and cool
then there were two green speckled frogs
Yum Yum

Two little speckled frogs
Sat on a speckled log
Eating some most delicious bugs
Yum Yum
One jumped into the pool
Where it was nice and cool
then there were one green speckled frog
Yum Yum

One little speckled frog
Sat on a speckled log
Eating some most delicious bugs
Yum Yum
One jumped into the pool
Where it was nice and cool
then there were no green speckled frogs
Yum Yum

Five Little Ducks

Five little Ducks went swimming one day
over the pond and far away
Mother Duck said
'Quack quack, quack quack'
But only four little ducks came back

Four little Ducks went swimming one day
over the pond and far away
Mother Duck said
'Quack quack, quack quack'
But only three little ducks came back

Three little Ducks went swimming one day
over the pond and far away
Mother Duck said
'Quack quack, quack quack'
But only two little ducks came back

Two little Ducks went swimming one day
over the pond and far away
Mother Duck said
'Quack quack, quack quack'
But only one little duck came back

One little Ducks went swimming one day
over the pond and far away
Mother Duck said
'Quack quack, quack quack'
No little ducks came swimming back

10 Green Bottles

10 green bottles hanging on the wall, 10 green bottles hanging on the wall, if 1 green bottle should accidentally fall, there'd be 9 green bottles hanging on the wall.

9 green bottles hanging on the wall, 9 green bottles hanging on the wall, if 1 green bottle should accidentally fall, there'd be 8 green bottles hanging on the wall.

8 green bottles hanging on the wall, 8 green bottles hanging on the wall, if 1 green bottle should accidentally fall, there'd be 7 green bottles hanging on the wall.

7 green bottles hanging on the wall, 7 green bottles hanging on the wall, if 1 green bottle should accidentally fall, there'd be 6 green bottles hanging on the wall.

6 green bottles hanging on the wall, 6 green bottles hanging on the wall, if 1 green bottle should accidentally fall, there'd be 5 green bottles hanging on the wall.

5 green bottles hanging on the wall, 5 green bottles hanging on the wall, if 1 green bottle should accidentally fall, there'd be 4 green bottles hanging on the wall.

4 green bottles hanging on the wall, 4 green bottles hanging on the wall, if 1 green bottle should accidentally fall, there'd be 3 green bottles hanging on the wall.

3 green bottles hanging on the wall, 3 green bottles hanging on the wall, if 1 green bottle should accidentally fall, there'd be 2 green bottles hanging on the wall.

2 green bottles hanging on the wall, 2 green bottles hanging on the wall, if 1 green bottle should accidentally fall, there'd be 1 green bottle hanging on the wall.

1 green bottle hanging on the wall, 1 green bottle hanging on the wall, if 1 green bottle should accidentally fall, there'd be NO green bottles hanging on the wall.

5 Fat Sausages

5 fat sausages sizzling in the pan
1 went POP
And then there were 4

4 fat sausages sizzling in the pan
1 went POP
And then there were 3

3 fat sausages sizzling in the pan
1 went POP
And then there were 2

2 fat sausages sizzling in the pan
1 went POP
And then there were 1

1 fat sausage sizzling in the pan
1 went POP
And then there were none

5 Currant Buns

5 currant buns in the baker's shop
Fat and round with sugar on top
. . . . came along with a penny one day
and bought a currant bun and took it away

Rap Rhymes

How Many Pupils

How many pupils are here today
How many pupils are here today
One, two, three, four
Is that all, or are there more?
Five, six, seven, eight
How many more by the garden gate
1 more, 2 more, 3 more 4?
That's how many are here today

Count With Me

Count with me, 1, 2, 3
Count with me, 1, 2, 3
Take my hand and shake it hard
Point to the number on the card
Is it a 1 (yes/no)
Is it a 2 (yes/no)
Is it a 3 (yes/no)

Let's count together 2, 3, 4
Count with me 2, 3, 4
Take my hand and shake it hard
Point to a number on the card
Is it a 2 (yes/no)
Is it a 3 (yes/no)
Is it a 4 (yes/no)

Let's count together 3, 4, 5
Count with me 3, 4, 5
Take my hand and shake it hard
Point to a number on the card
Is it a 3 (yes/no)
Is it a 4 (yes/no)
Is it a 5 (yes/no)

Let's count together 4, 5, 6
Count with me 4, 5, 6
Take my hand and shake it hard
Point to a number on the card
Is it a 4 (yes/no)
Is it a 5 (yes/no)
Is it a 6 (yes/no)

Let's count together 5, 6, 7
Count with me 5, 6, 7
Take my hand and shake it hard
Point to a number on the card
Is it a 5 (yes/no)
Is it a 6 (yes/no)
Is it a 7 (yes/no)

Clap your hands and wiggle your fingers

Tune: Bobby Shaftoe

Let's count together 7, 8, 9

Count with me 7, 8, 9
Take my hand and shake it hard
Point to a number on the card
Is it a 7 (yes/no)
Is it a 8 (yes/no)
Is it a 9 (yes/no)

Let's count together 8, 9, 10
Count with me 8, 9, 10
Take my hand and shake it hard
Point to a number on the card
Is it a 8 (yes/no)
Is it a 9 (yes/no)
Is it a 10 (yes/no)

Ten famous footballers

Two famous footballers were lying on the floor along came another two and then there were four,
Four famous footballers were practising their kicks along came another two and then there were six,
Six famous footballers were running a bit late along came another two and then there were eight,
Eight famous footballers ran to their den along came another two and then there were ten,
How many footballers were in our team? 2–4–6–8–10

1, 2, 3, 4, 5, once I caught a fish alive

1, 2, 3, 4, 5, once I caught a fish alive
6, 7, 8, 9, 10, then I let it go again
Why did you let it go
because it bit my finger so
Which finger did it bite
10, 9, 8, 7, 6, I will catch a fish with sticks
5, 4, 3, 2, 1, that didn't work so I got my gun . . . BANG!!

Five Speckled Frogs backwards

No little speckled frogs sat on a speckled log
Eating no most delicious grubs yum yum,
Out jumped a silly fool who thought I am so cool
Then there was one green speckled frog glub glub,
One little speckled frog sat on a speckled log
Eating a most delicious grub yum yum,
He jumped up like a dog – I need another frog,
Then there were two green speckled frogs glub glub,
Two little speckled frogs sat on a speckled log,
Eating some most delicious grubs yum yum,
Out jumped a speckled frog eating some Christmas log,
Then there were three green speckled frogs glub glub,
Three little speckled frogs sat on a speckled log,
Eating some most delicious grubs yum yum,
I want to see my dog – so I will call a frog,
Then there were four green speckled frogs,
Four little speckled frogs sat on a speckled log,
Eating some most delicious grubs yum yum,
Out jumped the baby frog on to the speckled log
Then there were five green speckled frogs glub glub.

To the tune of Frere Jacques

We love numbers
We love numbers
Numbers are fun
Numbers are fun
Let's all count together
Let's all count together
Start with one
Start with one

The following needs to be sung quite quickly
1 2 3 4 5 6 7   8 9 10   8 9 10

10 9 8 7 6 5   10 9 8 7 6 5   4 3 2 1   4 3 2 1

Where is zero
Where is zero
It comes before one
It comes before one
Let's remember zero
Let's remember zero
It comes before one
It comes before one

No currant buns in a baker's shop

No currant buns in a baker's shop
What shall we do? said Mrs Mop,
We'll call on X who'll bring us a bun,
With that bun we'll have one.

One currant bun in a baker's shop,
What shall we do? said Mrs Mop,
We'll call on X who'll bring us one that's new,
With that bun we will have two.

Two currant buns in a baker's shop,
What shall we do? said Mrs Mop,
We'll call on X who'll bring one for me,
With that bun we will have three.

Three currant buns in a baker's shop,
What shall we do? said Mrs Mop,
We'll call on X who'll open the door,
With that bun we will have four.

Four currant buns in a baker's shop,
What shall we do? said Mrs Mop,
We'll call on X whose bun is alive,
With that bun we will have five.
Five currant buns are back in the shop,
Thank goodness for that, said Mrs Mop.

Appendix 2: Other recommended resources

Mental Warm-up Activities, published by Ginn. ISBN 0-602-29022-8.

A Feel for Number. Activities for Number Recovery Programme. Published by Beam. ISBN 1-874-09932-4.

Number in the Nursery and Reception. A framework for Supporting and Assessing Number Learning. Published by Beam. ISBN 1-874-09969-3.

Learning Mathematics in the Nursery. published by Beam. Desirable Approaches. ISBN 1-874-09963-4.

Range of tactile resources such as counting books, farms, floor puzzles, number rhyme books.

Character sets for 5 little frogs, ducks, etc., available from Music Education Supplies Ltd, 101 Banstead Road South, Sutton, Surrey SM2 5LH, telephone 020 8770 3866.

Also early years equipment from Primary Learning Ltd, telephone 01892 546309, such as wall hangings on number colour, shape.

Example of rhymes counting activities can be found in *Mental Maths*, published by Cambridge University Press, ISBN 0-521-57764-0, and *Talking Points* by Anita Strakar, published by Cambridge University Press, ISBN 0-521-447585.

Appendix 3: Glossary of terms

Add	To combine two or more quantities to form another quantity. The symbol for this combination is 1 (plus).
Addition	The operation of combining two or more quantities.
Angle	Amount of turn, commonly in degrees.
Area	The size of a surface, which can be flat or curved.
Capacity	The measure of the amount something can hold.
Cardinal number	A number which denotes its size but not its order (e.g. 1, 2, 3 . . .).
Circle	A two-dimensional (flat) shape: all points are the same, fixed distance from the centre.
Classification	Sorting objects/numbers according to their properties or attributes.
Combining	Putting together (e.g. adding).
Comparing	Looking for similarities or differences in the properties of things.
Concept	An idea, especially one generalised from various instances.
Cone	A three-dimensional solid which has a circular base and tapers to a point at the top.
Count	To find out exactly 'how many'.
Counting	The operation of finding out exactly 'how many'.
Criteria	The rules applied when classifying.

Cube	A regular three-dimensional solid the faces of which are six squares.
Cuboid	A solid which has rectangles for all six of its faces.
Difference	The amount by which one quantity is greater or less than another.
Digit	A single figure used to represent a number (0, 1, 2, 3, 4, 5, 6, 7, 8, 9).
Direction	The course a person/object takes to get to a given destination (e.g. left, right, forward, backward).
Grouping	Making collections of objects by classifying.
Length	The property of how long something is in one direction.
Mass	The amount of matter in a body.
Mathematical pattern	A pattern which develops according to one clear rule.
Measuring	The operation of finding out 'how much' by comparing.
Movement	Change in position (e.g. forward, backward, to the left/right, on to, off, underneath.
Number	1. The idea of quantity, or how many. 2. The symbol used to represent how many.
Number line	A straight line on which numbers are marked.
Numeral	The symbol which represents a number.
One-to-one correspondence	A relationship between two sets of objects. Each object in the first set is paired with one object in the second set. Each object in the second set is paired with one object in the first set.
Operation	The action of combining and/or partitioning.
Ordinal number	A number indicating the position in a sequence (e.g. first, second, third . . .).
Partitioning	Separating into parts.
Pattern	An arrangement of things according to a rule.

Patterning	Developing or creating a mathematical pattern.
Position	The place occupied by a person or thing (e.g. on, in, under, behind, in front of).
Properties	The ways in which things behave and the qualities they possess.
Pyramid	A three-dimensional solid shape with flat faces that has a polygon (many sided shape) as a base. The sides are triangles which meet at a common point at the top.
Rectangle	A two-dimensional shape with four straight sides. All angles are 90°.
Shape	A closed region two-dimensional or closed two-dimensional body.
Sign	A symbol usually representing an operation to be performed (e.g. $+, -, \times, \div$).
Solid	A three-dimensional figure having length, breadth and depth, (e.g. cube, sphere, pyramid).
Sphere	A three-dimensional solid: all points on the surface are a given fixed distance from the centre.
Square	A two-dimensional shape. A rectangle with all sides equal in length.
Subtract	The operation of taking away, or finding the difference between two quantities.
Sum	The result of combining or adding two of more numbers or quantities together.
Symbol	Something that stands for another: a sign (e.g. $+, -, \times, \div$).
Time	A system of measuring continuous existence.
Triangle	A two-dimensional shape with three straight sides.
Weight	The force acting on a mass due to gravity.
Zero	The number which represents a set that has no numbers in it.